Dedica

I dedicate this book to God, Jesus, Spirit, my Guides and Angels. God is my creator; my father and I honor him in this work every day. He is the reason I serve. Jesus is my friend and is always by my side supporting my journey. Spirit honors me the way I honor them. They work hand and hand with me to help their loved ones. I am always grateful for their help and honor their lives through the messages I pass. My Guides are with me all the time. They support, love and protect me. We are on this journey together and I couldn't ask for a better Guide team. They are my family, my teachers and my friends. We are in service together to serve God. I honor them and the work we do together. I couldn't do this work without them. They keep me grounded and focused on the bigger picture of what this work is all about. We are here to work together to share God's love and messages from Spirit. We are working together as a unit to honor and pass messages to offer peace and give proof of the other side. They are my biggest cheerleader's and I trust the way they guide me. They are the ones that gave me the guidance for the stories you will hear about in this book. I just listened and honored what they asked me to do. They are the reason I wrote this book. My experiences over the years have been beautifully miraculous. I am grateful for them every day. They are my soul family. I will continue to honor them and the work we do together for the rest of my life. I welcome and work with several angels as well. They are always giving me love and protection, so I dedicate this book to my whole team from God, to Jesus, to the loved ones in Spirit, to my Guides and the Angels. Thank you for loving me.

Table of Contents

Gifts From Spirit

By

Kelly Schloer

Answering My Calling

Ever since I was a young girl I could feel God's hand on my heart. Even at the age of thirteen I knew and felt his love for me. Those memories were so long ago, but I think of them fondly. I spent part of my summers at a church camp, whimsically named Camp Hashawha in Westminster, Maryland. I spent weeks there in those formative years between the ages of eleven and fourteen. As anyone who knows, these years are not easy ones. Like any adolescent girl I felt vulnerable, uncertain and a little worried. The future was a scary place. What was I going to be when I grew up? What did my future hold? While at camp it seemed that dreams danced around in my head, untethered by the day to day struggles of growing up. Perhaps it was that nature is a grounding place and that surrounded by the beauty around me, I was free to open myself up to all the changes my life was going through. Adolescence is, by it's very nature, a transformation, the physical changing of a girl to a young woman. I was no different than anyone else at that age but at camp I found a serenity and a oneness with the nature that surrounded me. It was that very connection to earth and nature that helped me to understand more of what my life was to become.

Camp allowed me to slow down, to focus on me or sometimes to focus on nothing at all. Away from the asphalt, the hustle and bustle of small town life I felt wild and free. A simple hike in the woods when I would stop by a stream and allow the gurgling of water to fill my spirit, became an interlude of peace. Or perhaps tilting my head up through the mottled sun streaming through the pine trees allowed me to see the world as it should be. Or maybe the feeling of walking through a sun drenched clearing, grasshoppers leading the way and that glorious fresh scent of pine and wild grasses. Most of us have experienced this, and to those who haven't, I invite you to try it. My camp memories are special to me and include camp fires, the sharp tang of wood smoke, good friends and singing around the fire at night. I remember singing "Kumbaya, my Lord", that old camp standard, but it took on a stronger meaning to me. Later I would read these words:

"Someone's singing Lord, kumbaya

Someone's laughing, Lord, kumbaya

Someone's crying, Lord, kumbaya

Someone's praying, Lord, kumbaya

Someone's sleeping, Lord, kumbaya

I found out later that this song was a song for an appeal to God to help those in need.

At the time, I had no idea how much these simple lyrics would mean to me and my future calling as a Medium. I was making tentative connections I didn't understand and wouldn't for years to come.

Some of my "camp" memories were standard ones, I suppose, but some seemed to be far more than arts and crafts and spooky camp stories. I vividly remember sitting on the bench under the pines watching two beautiful, majestic snow owls that were permanent camp residents. I felt a peace like nothing else I had ever felt before. I would sit there watching the owls as they watched me. They would knowingly regard me from the ancient pine branches and I would return their gazes, entranced at their beauty. In every turn of their heads, in every subtle move they made, I felt a sense of connection and belonging. I felt a belonging to God, to them, to the earth and to that very moment. Even at such a young age I knew I needed to stop and just breathe in those occasions of stillness. I felt the stillness in my mind and heart like no other time I had ever experienced. Even at the tender age of thirteen, I felt wise in that instant moment of surrender. It was as if I had found something so complete, so whole, so loving it couldn't be explained through just mere words. I found a connection with God, with Jesus and with Spirit. I could feel God's love and peace move through every part of my being. I knew then, in those moments, that I would forever be impacted by those experiences.

I surrendered to God that day, in the shade of the pines under the watchful eyes of those two owls. It was in the very act of surrendering that I realized this was a pivotal moment in my life and that allowed me to see that this was a new beginning. I also felt that if I was to grow and change and answer His call it would be in a way I hadn't thought of before. I felt something important was going to happen. But, as in most changes, I also wanted to remain in that moment forever. In my mind's eye, this bench, these snow owls would forever be something I would cherish in my soul. I remember, when I finished church camp that year, I was full of new questions and yes, even some answers. Every year I made my pilgrimage back to the snowy owls and I felt God's embrace and felt secure in His arms.

I have had this same conversation of surrender many times over the years with God. That memory, that moment, is the one that resonates in my heart and in my soul the most. I am so thankful for that sacred promise, those sacred words of surrender and the continued surrender I have given over the years. God spoke to me that day in words I can never truly express and it became the beginning of a further calling. But being called, and knowing exactly what that calling was is a very different thing. I waited patiently to find out what His plan was. What part I was to play in His plan? At one point, I thought I would be a pastor. What greater calling was there to work for Him in this way? To preach His word always seemed to be the pinnacle of service. It seemed the obvious choice! Of course, what we think and what He knows are not necessarily the same thing. Nevertheless, I accepted His call and agreed to give myself to being fully in His service.

Looking back now, I remember my childhood and realize the beginnings of my life as a sensitive. I was always in tune to things I didn't even realize. Sometimes it was just a feeling but many times I can remember knowing things before they happened. One monumental vision was the death of my grandfather.

I was only eleven. It was 8/9/1986 – no don't do the math! My parents had gone out together with friends. Just a pre-teen, but I suppose I was worldly compared to my little brother Jason, who was eight. I can remember sitting at the kitchen table with Jason and my younger brother, Justin was in the basement. At exactly 7:05 I turned to Jason and said. "There is something wrong with Grandpa."

Jason had answered, "Yeah, I know."

It was unsettling and disturbing and I had no one other than my little brother to talk to about it. Justin, in the basement would certainly not want to discuss it with his siblings. It worried me but I didn't understand what was wrong, just that something terrible would happen to my grandfather. A few hours later the phone rang and it was my grandmother who asked to speak with my parents. I explained they were out and she didn't tell me anymore than to have them call her. At almost 11 pm my mother returned her call. I was standing between my mom and my dad, my heart heavy and worried and waiting to hear what my grandmother would say, knowing the news would not be good. She told my mom that my dad's father had had a heart attack at 8pm that night and that he had passed away. I was astonished. The death of a dear grandfather was difficult to bear but more than that, was the fact that I had known about it, less than an hour before it actually happened! It wasn't a conscious thing, it was an intuitive knowing. This was the first real time I understood that I was different. I didn't feel any different than I had that morning, but the truth was undeniable. It was a lot for a child to comprehend.

As a child, I didn't understand this "knowing" of things that would happen as God's gift. It took me years before I understood His message. It wasn't until I became an adult that the message became clear. I don't know why God chose for me to come to this understanding later in life. Perhaps

God knew that at such a young age I wasn't ready either spiritually or emotionally to handle the responsibility and to take on the challenges and joys of such an unusual gift. Or maybe He wasn't ready for me? There is a time and a place for everything and mine was yet to be found. The strange part is, even when I became a young adult, a college student, a married woman – none of these milestones actually connected the dots for me. I just didn't understand with any clarity what I was to be called to do. And to be honest with myself, who would think that my gift, my *calling*, would be that of a Medium? Through the rediscovering of my childhood memories, I have come to understand I have had these gifts my whole life. Why did God see fit to give me gifts and not allow me to use them? As frustrating as that was, I could have stepped into being a Medium - years before I did, but I waited to hear His message. I waited and wondered and prayed but none of my prayers showed me where my path would lay. But, as I said earlier, it was not my place to question His plan, I had to trust that when He thought the time was right, I would know.

This does not mean that I didn't live my life without His gift, I just didn't use it, the way I do now. I knew that I had guides, spirits who truly guided me through my life and I learned to trust their gentle prods or even robust kicks when I didn't take the hint. I learned to listen to them and to follow what they said, even if I didn't understand fully what it meant. I needed to honor them and through them honor God. This included where I was to start my service.

You see, my husband, Jeff and I lived in Maine. We fell in love with it years before when visiting Bar Harbor on our first anniversary. We had no intentions of leaving. Maine was our home. A few months prior to finally understanding what God and Spirit wanted me to do I found myself under a doctor's care and with significant health problems. It became clear I could no longer physically work a normal job. Jeff and I went from two incomes to one and found ourselves in a small one-bedroom apartment. I was devastated, scared and worried. I couldn't help but ponder on that nagging question, now what? Then out of of the blue, like a beacon of hope, my message came. Guided through Spirit and my faith in God I knew my message was clear. My guides told me that it was time to step into my calling as a Medium.

That in itself was quite the surprise but they didn't stop there.

I was also compelled to leave Jeff in Maine and fly to my home state of Maryland! I was assured by my spiritual guides that all would be well, that Maryland was where I would be starting my service as a Medium. I was also told that Jeff would get a job offer in Maryland and that the company would pay for half the move. My guides were very specific about this and by then I had learned that when Spirit tells you something, you must honor and follow their advice. I knew that I was to return home to Maryland to start my business as a Medium and not look back. I was supposed to get on a plane and leave Jeff in Maine. Through Spirit, I was also told that we would have a house to live in right away. I had no idea how Spirit would manage that, still I had come to trust my guides and my God. My guides were clear - as was the message.

Jeff came home in the middle of March after a long day at work and I told him, we needed to talk. Famous last words for any man but Jeff quietly sat on the floor in front of me and listened. I told him what I was shown, the trip to Maryland. The job offers. The house we were to have. The start up as a Medium and the fact that he was to stay in Maine. I trusted my guides and I loved my husband but even the most devout, loving caring man should bat an eye at such an outlandish idea.

Not Jeff.

Jeff got off the floor and posted on Facebook that we were moving back to Maryland. Within five minutes his cousin offered her house for us to live in. Soon after, he got the job offer and the company paid for half the move. I can not say that I loved him anymore than I already did but his attitude and belief in me, just solidified our love. Jeff never waivered at my outlandish ideas. He trusted me. I trusted Spirit. And so it happened. Spirit was taking me for a ride and I better hold on to my hat!

This all came to fruition because I listened and trusted. I also was blessed with an amazing husband who blindly followed where I lead, despite him not having Spirit "talking" to him. If I said it was so, it was because Spirit said it was. Then it was. It's amazing what can happen when we slow down and listen and trust God's path for us and our life.

With God's blessing and the support of my husband I took this incredible leap of faith. I knew I had to honor God and my calling. Nervous and anxious with excitement I remember boarding the plane from Maine to Maryland. I put my complete trust in God's hands for my path to come. I took a deep breath as I took off not knowing what to expect, but hopeful for what God had in store for my life. I remember watching the clouds out the window as I flew from my Maine home to my new life in Maryland. Thoughts of all the "what ifs" flooded me. What if the job fell through with Jeff? What if my business did not thrive? I didn't think so. My guides can be pretty adamant about such things. Yet, I had no real choice and once again I centered myself and realized that my guides had never been wrong before! Thankfully, it was a short flight, so I didn't have too much time to dwell on all of my unanswered questions or exhaust much energy on my human emotions. When the wheels of the jet touched ground at BWI all doubt left me. It was as if I was seeing clearly for the first time. I knew I was where I need to be. God needed me to come and help in the state I grew up in.

I was instantly happy and filled with a warmth of loving energy that overwhelmed me, I was home. Home not just in the sense of being in my home state. I felt as if I had truly come *home* to that love and peacefulness I had as that young girl of thirteen. To my snow owls and the peace of the forest. I felt as if I truly found myself suspended in a moment of peace. It was a recognizing of my own Spirit, the oneness of God and that He wanted me to feel - to *know*- this was where I belonged.

From that day until now I have grown in my own faith and abilities. I have learned to slow down and just listen and trust. Trusting the guidance and words given to me over the years has led me to write this book. I hope you find peace, love and connection with the re-telling of these remarkable short stories. They are just a small part of the bigger journey I intend to continue with you and hope you follow with me. I was blessed to be a part of the people and events I am sharing with you and am happy to do it. This is a journey guided in love, faith, trust and it has allowed me to give proof of the afterlife. They are stories of connections I have made with loved ones on the other side, to give comfort to their loved ones here. I hope these stories inspire you to be open to the connections that your loved ones are always making with you. My passion is to help you gain a new

renewed faith and open your heart to the miraculous gifts from spirit.

Dragonfly of Hope

As a Medium, I have learned that there are many symbols that help guide us. One such symbol is the dragonfly. It represents change and is a sign of guidance sent to loved ones here. It is also a sign of celebration of a new life and change to come and trusting in the process of the transformations coming in your life. It is a sign of support for your journey. The dragonfly reminds us to slow down and trust the timing of things. Trust your loved ones are guiding your direction. The dragonfly can also be a simple message of love that you are being watched over. It does have other meanings as well, but of these, directional guidance is the strongest meaning.

In this story of the message passed to Debbie and her young daughter Alex, you will come to understand the importance of the sign of the dragonfly. The dragonfly is not only an important sign to Debbie and Alex and from their loved one, it is also a directional sign from Alex's dad.

As a Medium I am always in service to God. I am always guided in all I do as well. I trust the advice given to me by my guides. I never know what the outcome will be, but I honor what I'm given. So, even when I'm asked to do something of which I can't even begin to understand why, I listen, trust and follow through and then I find myself amazed at the incredible outcomes. A few days before meeting Debbie and her daughter Alex at an upcoming reading, I felt very drawn to a dragonfly necklace. I looked at the necklace for some time and my heart felt so much peace. I knew it would be important but didn't know how important it would be. Still, I trusted my guides and purchased the necklace. I had no idea why or what it meant, nor did I know who for, but they were very sure I needed to have it.

Two days before I saw Debbie and Alex, I was walking through my house and heard a message. Yes, I get messages from my guides even when walking through my own home! I heard my guide say "Use the bag sitting in the dining room with a picture of the Eiffel tower on it." Then I saw a picture given to me by my guides of that dragonfly necklace. I knew they were asking me to put the necklace in that bag. I had no idea who I would be giving it to, but trusted what they were showing me in that moment. I trusted God, trusted them and knew it was going to impact great change. I felt it would speak to someone's heart in a special way. I was scheduled to do a group reading where people had purchased tickets to see me to have a chance to connect. Just before I left for the group that day it was placed on my heart to take the gift along. Again, there is no discussion with Spirit, I do what I am told to do and then quietly wait for the answers to arrive. Yes, they surprise even me!

When I arrived at the space in downtown Baltimore, I gave the gift to my husband to hold. Not knowing who the gift would go I had nothing else to say and Jeff, being Jeff, just nodded and held onto the little Eiffel tower bag with it's dragonfly necklace. I was left to wonder who I would give it to or even if I was to really have brought it in the first place. I believed there was a reason because my guides had told me so, but I had a roomful of guests to read and I had no idea who would be the recipient of the dragonfly necklace. It is a very strange feeling to purchase a gift randomly for someone you don't know! I was as in the dark as everyone else. This may all seem a little daunting but this is just par for the course for me. All I could do was to trust in my guides and God to lead me to the right person. I am always excited to pass messages and offer healing and this was a special gift. I was thrilled to be able to be a part in whatever was to happen next. The message I was about to pass on from Debbie's loved one and the message I received after from Debbie will stay in my heart forever.

A gentleman by the name of John stepped in and he said to me "Kelly get the gift". When I mentioned his name Debbie and Alex raised their hands. I walked over with the gift and in front of the crowd told everyone how I was guided to the gift and the bag it went into. As I started passing messages from John, he told me his daughter was fourteen. John told me his daughter had been having a hard time since his passing. His words to his daughter were so comforting and healing. I could feel Debbie and especially Alex's anxiety melting away as John's words of comfort came from my voice. His statements and validation were so powerful. I did not realize *how* powerful until afterwards when speaking with Debbie.

In the process of the message, Alex opened the gift from her dad, John. When she pulled out the necklace I heard her gasp and a moment later she and Debbie were crying. They told me at that moment that they knew John had been sending them dragonflies. They had been seeing dragonflies everywhere. Even in places that shouldn't HAVE dragonflies! They knew in their hearts it was his sign for them in spirit, letting them know he was with them. There was a gradual relaxation of Alex's shoulders, a deep breath and then so very slowly, I saw Alex smile. It was tentative at first and I could see through the tears the slow grin of a happy teenager, then a smile - brilliant and warm and full of love. Her daddy was there. He was always there and he was watching out for her. When I saw the smile on Alex's face it meant so much to me. I was honored to give her just a few minutes to have that connection with her dad.

After I finished reading the group I was surprised to see strangers come up to Alex, to hold her close and cling to her, hugs of joy from people who maybe hadn't even gotten a reading. It was incredible to see. This group of strangers had been privy to an emotional and intimate part of Alex and Debbie's life and their reaction was to love and hold a mother and her daughter. There was no pretense, no anger they hadn't been read, just people who had experienced an amazing gift. They had seen the power of Spirit change a little girl's life. And me? I was just the go between! That being said, it made me proud and honored to have been able to help this troubled teenager "see" her dad again.

The next day I received a message of thanks from Debbie. It was one I was not prepared for and it touched my soul in such a deep way, I will cherish the thankfulness of that message always.

Debbie proceeded to tell me that Alex had been struggling since her dad's passing and was having a difficult time. She then told me she hadn't seen her daughter really smile in three years. She told me she knew the reading would forever change Alex's life. Those words were so powerful when I read them that it shook me a bit. How had I done this? How had I managed to make it all happen? She then referred to the black and white Eiffel tower bag. She told me that two weeks before they had started to change Alex's bedroom. (A teenager's prerogative!!) They had just hung Paris curtains in her bedroom, with the Eiffel tower as the

main theme! Alex had wanted to change her little girl room to the more
sophisticated grown- up motif and into a Paris theme and so they did!

Weeks before their message from me. I was in
shock. To think all that I did was trust my guidance. My guides had me
purchase the dragonfly necklace. I was told to put that dragonfly necklace
into that bag. I was shown that I needed to bring it to the upcoming
reading. How is that possible? How had I done this? How had I managed
to make it all happen? The truth is, I didn't make anything happen, I was
just the conduit between John and his daughter and wife.

Alex's dad, John, was behind the whole thing. He knew they were
recognizing the sign of the dragonfly from him. He also knew they had just
started to change Alex's bedroom. He knew they were coming to my see
me. He could also see Alex's pain and knew she needed that
message.

How he convinced my guides to coerce me into buying a dragonfly
necklace and putting it in an Eiffel Tower gift bag, I still don't know. But I
do know that a message of hope from a dad saying "I'm here, and I'm
helping you through all of this, and I love you," came through that night in
Baltimore. A beautiful connection was made because I stopped, listened to
the guidance, and trusted what was asked of me. John had reached out from
the other side with the sign of a dragonfly for hope, guidance and direction.
His love for his young daughter whose life was changing was a message of
everlasting hope. John knew she needed to know he was still guiding her
on her journey. I wish Alex further peace and connections with her dad in

the years to come, and for me? Well, I stopped took a few seconds and thanked God. I thanked God for the gifts he has given me to do the work that I do and the unique privilege of sharing the joy and hope of reuniting a father and daughter on a special night with visions of the Eiffel tower in Baltimore.

Signs from the Ocean

I love being a Medium and traveling to other areas to help as much as I can. My traveling allows me to go to so many wonderful places, but the ocean has always been one of my favorite spots. There is always something special about being by the ocean for me. The sound of the waves, the smell of the salt air, the breeze gently blowing across my face. All of these bring me such an overwhelming sense of peace. Many people feel this way, the rhythms of the ocean can allow a higher state of peacefulness of mind, body and soul. This is nothing new. For millennium, the ocean, the tides and our connections to the sea have always been important to many different cultures. Mother Ocean feeds us, protects us and offers us a deeper connection to nature. The simplicity of the sound of the ocean, the rhythm of the tides and the greater overall feeling of peace that being near the ocean brings. Every wave breaks differently, just like the paths of our lives. Each wave is part of the ocean but is unique in its journey. As the ocean ebbs and flows, it releases the tension of our souls. There are high tides and low tides, there are times when we are challenged and buffeted by the breakers and other times we can rest in the lull of the waves. These observations are my own but they are universal. My client Diane is someone who is as they say, is a water baby, a soul drawn to the ocean. This next story recounts her love of the ocean, the much needed guidance and love from her father and how I helped her to understand his love.

I had planned a weekend at the beach in Ocean City, MD. Ocean City is a busy beach from Memorial day to Labor day. There is a constant hum in the air and the sound of children laughing, playing skee ball and revelers enjoying all the town has to offer.

Fenwick Island in nearby Delaware, is a tourist spot in it's own right but it draws a different type of person. For someone for whom the bright lights, traffic and noise and excitement of OC is too much, Fenwick may offer a gentle alternative. The quietness of Fenwick Island feeds the soul in a way the boisterousness of Ocean City can not. We planned a two-night event in Ocean City, where people purchased tickets for one, or both nights to see me. Most people came with family and friends and stayed at the hotel overlooking the ocean and Diane was one of the attendees. It was a beautiful weekend getaway full of blue skies and the sound of the pounding surf.

The day before my first group, I went out to lunch and did some shopping with my husband and friends. As we were out exploring, I felt very drawn to go into a locally owned storefront in Fenwick. It was a quaint shop off the beaten path on the less busy Bayside portion of the

town. Outside there was an eclectic group of ceramics and fountains. One

of my favorite kinds of places to shop, but not a place to look for a gift for

someone I would be reading. That wasn't my intention. I in fact, found

myself purchasing lotus flower decorations to add my own home. In the

process of shopping my, eye caught some signs shaped to look like a

paddle or maybe an oar. These were not in the window or anywhere I

would naturally look for them. I actually had to walk through the store and

to the left to find these unusual decorations. We were in the shop longer

than expected because I found myself once again, listening to my guidance

from Spirit. Apparently my lotus flowers were not the only thing on the

shopping list. As I walked around I had a father presence step in and tell

me that his name was Arthur. He said to me to look at the signs hanging on

the wall. I looked up and above my head was a sign shaped like a paddle

board with Fenwick Island written across it. My guides told me that that

sign was a gift from Arthur to his daughter. I asked for assistance to get it

down and felt a beautiful rush of energy when I held it. It made me excited

at the thought of giving it as a gift.

I was so anxious about getting to my group, just to have a chance to

hand the paddle sign to Arthur's daughter. The evening was a beautiful one

full of validations and messages of hope. About half way through the reading that night Arthur stepped in again, much as he had while I was shopping. As soon I felt him I walked back to Jeff and toward the gift I had purchased. I picked up the gift for Diane. Her dad's message explained to me how it was a dream of Diane's to live by the ocean. His Fenwick paddle sign to her was the validation of where she would eventually be settling. It was not only an answer for her, but Arthur knew in Diane's heart that she needed to make the move. That she needed the peace, serenity and healing power of the ocean. He told her it would take a few years but acknowledged it would come. Arthur told me that she needed to start "taking care of herself" and that she needed to start taking smaller trips to the ocean. That the ocean was her healing place and that eventually, it would be her home. I could see not only the joy in her eyes, but I could feel the peace it gave her.

The following weekend, I received a private message from Diane. She told me that she took the sign home and hung it over her bed as reminder of what was to come. A promise from her father and a visual reminder that she needed to continue to work toward her goal of living by the sea.

I have seen Diane since then and she now enjoys one weekend a month at the ocean and is slowly making the adjustments to make it her retirement destination. She understood why her dad told her she needed to have more peace and take better care of herself. She realized that the ocean was where she needed to be.

She is now doing just that.

I can't wait until that Fenwick sign from a tiny shop outside of the bay, graces her new home at the ocean one day. What a beautiful, simple reminder she will have of her Dad's love hanging on the wall of her new home.

A Mother's Love

The sign of the cardinal is one of most recognized signs that a loved one is present and watching over us. This beautiful bird with the striking red plumage is more than just a bright splash of red against the green of the forest or the backdrop of a snowy winter day. The cardinal has long been known as a sign of a loved one being near for over a century. This bright, red bird has been known as a sign of good health, happiness, harmony and family. These cheerful, hardy birds are great parents, with both mom and dad taking care of their brood. That may be one of the reasons why it is strongly associated with the love of family. Some of the meanings attached to cardinals include protection and for many of us, this bird reminds us that our loved ones are watching. The word cardinal comes from the Latin word "cardo" which means hinge. The cardinal, like the hinges on a door, allows for the connection to the doorway between Spirit and those here on earth and as such, is a sign of communication. Many people talk to cardinals when they see them - feeling that their messages will be heard by their loved ones in spirit. I too, have a remarkable story involving cardinals. I hope you find this as inspirational as I did.

Several years ago, I was on tour in Texas. I was lucky enough to read a beautiful young girl named Ashley. As often happens, her loved ones wanted to connect to her and I was the conduit for their connection. Not surprisingly, her mother Mary, came through to talk to her lovely daughter. Mary had passed away a few years before from cancer and she was as anxious to connect with her daughter as Ashley was to speak with her. Mom came through, loud and clear and wanted to be heard.

I remember Mary being one of the first messages of Spirit to come through that night and how important Mary felt that she needed to show her daughter how much Ashley was loved. The detail Mary gave was exceptional, so much so, that even though it was years ago, I can remember vividly some of the validations that came through. Her mom began with details of her cancer and her passing - along with specific dates that were important to Ashley and her mother. She congratulated Ashley on her one-year anniversary, to a man that Mary couldn't possibly know that Ashley had even married! For Ashley, not having her mother around for such a special day was very difficult. What little girl doesn't dream of her wedding day surrounded by a mother's gentle touch and the joy that her baby has taken such a momentous and loving step? Ashley didn't ask any questions, she just listened as her mother spoke. There was no need to, as Mary knew what was in Ashley's heart and the things she needed most to hear. Mary told me the exact date of Ashley's marriage and through Spirit she showed me that her daughter had been glowing and so beautiful on the day she wed. Mary then began to describe how she accompanied Ashley down the aisle in Spirit. She told me that Ashley had taken some of the lace from her own wedding dress and had sown it into hers. A loving remembrance of the mother she lost. Mary also showed me the special pieces of her jewelry Ashley wore to honor her mother on that beautiful day. Mary also validated that Ashley tucked her mother's handkerchief into the flowers of her bouquet. Mary was so honored that her daughter chose such loving, sentimental ways to honor Mary's life and to honor Ashley's own new beginnings in ways that were important to Ashley. This momentous occasion was something that Mary would never have missed and she wanted Ashley to know it. She wanted her daughter to know she had been present to see her wed the love of her life. Her mom's validations proved that she was indeed there. To see Ashley's face light up with the knowledge that her mom had been present was so joyful. Then, as only Spirit would know, she told me that Ashley and her husband were trying to get pregnant. Imagine, Ashley's surprise at this validation! It was true! It was then that Mary told me she would be an angel for her daughter's baby.

Mary needed to let Ashley know that their's was a bond of more than just the special one of mother and daughter. They were best friends. She conveyed all of this and more to Ashley and Ashley was overwhelmed with the connection between her and her mom. A connection I was privileged to help forge.

It was then that Mary asked me to tell Ashley to watch out for cardinals. They were to be a special sign from mother to daughter, a peaceful, gentle reminder that Mary's love would never die and that she would forever be watching over Ashley. The cardinal, a sign of protection, family and love would forever bind Ashley to Mary and that she should know the bright and cheery bird's presence was more than just a chance encounter.

Throughout the rest of the reading, Mary went on to say many other things that offered peace to Ashley. The bond of love Ashley felt with her mom would forever stay with her and her mother's protection and closeness to her daughter was revealed the longer I spoke. Later, I received a wonderful message from Ashley letting me know how much healing the reading had offered. She spoke of renewed faith and love for her mother and how her messages had impacted Ashley's life. Then, to prove the point, Ashley told me since the validations she received during her reading, she was seeing more cardinals than ever before and was feeling her mom's presence in her life in a special way. How wonderful to be a part of the sharing of Spirit to a young woman who desperately missed and needed the connection with her mom.

Love is everlasting. Our love bonds and connects us with our loved ones in spirit. The symbol of the cardinal will always remain a sign of Ashley's mom's love and protection for her. In this instance, the cardinal was truly the "hinge" that opened the door to allow Ashley to know how this beautiful, red, spunky bird will always be a representation of the connection between the other side and here.

A Welcoming New Addition

Children are one of God's greatest gifts. The blessing of a new baby to the family can bring so much joy. The excitement and anticipation of not only the new parents, but the knowledge that family can create everlasting bonds is palpable. We create bonds with those we love here and those bonds continue on the other side. You see, our loved ones on the other side have bonded with us before they passed through love and those attachments are strong and everlasting. Mere death doesn't break them and they will always remain between our deceased loved ones and those that they love. This is especially true when it comes to new babies joining the family. It is through that love that the other side connects with the new, younger generation. How many times have we thought when expecting a new child...I wish that Grandma was here to celebrate our joyous new child? The thing is, she is! They all are! They are always watching over the family as a whole. Our loved ones continue to send prayers and blessings for all they touched in life and even those not yet born. They also know when a new baby will be gifted to the family from God and are excited to share the news with young, hopeful parents. I am about to tell you a remarkable story about just this.

My husband and I were staying in Baltimore for a few days while I was in the area helping family and friends. Just before a group one night, literally minutes before I left to read them, I was walking through the kitchen and heard from one of my guides. I heard the words "Go to Lifeway and buy a baby present." Lifeway is a local store and one I sometimes frequent, so I of course followed their advice and headed on a shopping expedition for baby presents! A strange occurrence you might say, but not for one connected in Spirit to the other side. Again, as I stated before, when my guides ask me to do something I listen. I left the house and headed straight to the store. I knew the lay of the land at Lifeways and knew they had a gift section for babies on the right. I already felt in my heart I needed to get some type of stuffed animal. I searched through the tumble of plush animals until I found a beautiful white lamb that played "Jesus Loves Me" I knew without saying that it was perfect. Perfect for whom? I had no idea but it was exactly what I wanted, or shall I say, what Spirit wanted. I went to the register and purchased a bag and tissue paper and carefully placed the little white lamb in the bag. I was so excited! Purchasing gifts for someone doesn't always happen, but when it does the anticipation of who will receive it is incredibly exciting! Who would get the dear little lamb?

When I arrived at my group I walked in with the bag and Jeff grinned at me when I placed it in front of him on the table. He had been here before and just like me he knew it would be an interesting night! We are both like kids in a candy shop when this happens, giddy with excitement over the recipient's unexpected present. No one knows who will be chosen to receive a token from the other side and Jeff and I just sit back and watch it unfold. Well, Jeff does the sitting and I do the talking!

My very first message that night was a grandfather by the name of Henry. He conveyed to me that his granddaughter was here. Then Henry clearly told me to get the gift and place it in front of a young woman seated patiently waiting to be read. Her face was priceless when I told her that Henry said there was a new baby joining the family. Her first response was that it wasn't her! The deep blush and snort of slightly embarrassed laughter caused the whole room to chuckle. She then insisted no one she knew was pregnant and that it didn't belong to her. She was pleasant but firm, there were no babies in and around her future! Now of course not only do I honor Spirit, but I trust what they know more than anyone else here on this plane does, so I just told her to keep it, that it was for her, or someone she knew. I could also see Henry smiling and shaking his head indulgently as if he was holding back a great secret but could no longer do it anymore. Henry assured me eventually his granddaughter would understand. Henry than had me tell her that his job was that of a guardian for the new baby and that he took his job seriously. Slightly confused, she accepted the gift but I could clearly see she had no idea what in the heck was going on. I went on to honor the rest of his message, she accepted this as well with graciousness and kindness. She didn't understand it all but was more than happy to hear her grandfather. I worked through the rest of the room receiving and communicating messages of peace to the others there. About twenty minutes before I was done, Henry's granddaughter tentatively raised her hand. She then told me that she had been texting messages to family members trying to figure out the information about the baby. One of the people she contacted was her Uncle Charles. When asked point blank about a new baby, he acquiesced in the face of absolute truth, and told her that her cousin was pregnant! Her cousin had not shared the news with the family and was waiting for the "right" time.

Apparently Henry thought the time was now!

When the young woman shared the news with the whole room I just smiled and enjoyed the happiness and good wishes from the group. I stood in that excited room, flooded with thankfulness that I honored Henry's message. I was so blessed to have been able to hear him tell me to purchase the baby gift while walking through the kitchen, no less. Spirit does not seem to care if messages are sent in the kitchen, the car or when grocery shopping! I know it, acknowledge it and do my best to follow their direction. In true fashion, validation often comes when we least expect it. Henry's saga and that of the new baby would be re-visited again in another remarkable addition to well - this remarkable addition!

A few months later I was reading a group in a totally different area. I was passing a message to someone in the group. In the middle of the message, my guides lead me back to the night I spoke with Henry. They showed me pictures and reminded me of the night Henry came through. I felt in that instant, they were using this as a teaching moment. A part of a continued need for me to trust in their spiritual guidance. I interpreted it that the person I was reading at the time needed to trust what was being said and to believe in it. Then, my guides encouraged me to tell Henry's story. As I was towards the end of the story a hand went up. Let me remind you that I see thousands of people a year. It is rare occasion when I recognize someone. When I do, it is often because Spirit is involved. I stopped to honor the lady raising her hand but I did not recognize her. She then said to me she was the granddaughter of Henry, the person I gave the baby gift to. It came back to me then, Henry's need for me to buy the cute little lamb and then to give it to his granddaughter. What was she doing here? It had been months since her reading and it was in a completely different area of the state. She then proceeded to tell me and everyone that the great grandchild Henry insisted was coming and that he was watching over was born that very morning.

It takes a lot to leave me speechless, ask any of my friends, but right then I had no words!

I stood and just shook my head in amazement. It took me a few seconds to collect myself and my emotions. How blessed was I? How incredible my gift from God and how amazing that all of this came together. It was one of the greatest experiences I have had while doing this work. To think it all started with a simple message of buying a baby present. The coincidences were far too many for it to be simply fate. First, I was told to honor Spirit by buying the gift, giving the gift and passing the message at the first reading. Then, at the second reading, Henry's granddaughter had to buy a ticket to see me. It had to be purchased ahead of time, most of the time I sell out. How did she happen to buy a ticket for a group on a day that her cousin was to deliver her little baby? I was shown by my guides to share the story of Henry and his granddaughter while reading another group of people, something that really made no sense as Henry came through months ago. That validation came full circle back to that first message. Stars aligning? Cosmic karma? All I can say is the answer is Spirit. Spirit moving through me, through Henry's granddaughter and through the tiniest of young lives. It was truly an incredible experience for everyone in the room that night.

Once again I was lead into that leap of faith, of believing and trusting in what is heard, felt and seen. To those reading this, trust that your loved ones are reaching out to make the same guiding connections that Henry did with me. Was all of that aligned and pre-planned, as they say, from the other side? Absolutely. It is astonishing how much of Spirit touches our lives. So, my message to you in this recounting of Henry's message is that we need to trust what we feel, hear and see. I know Henry is a proud great grandfather in heaven, guarding and protecting his new little charge. Your loved ones are proud of you as well and they are watching all of us with their combined knowledge and love. Trust in their connections and your experiences with them. They are truly blessings and if we open our hearts to them, we are able to feel the joy and love they have for us in this world.

Butterfly Kisses

I was going back to the ocean to read another group. It seemed an obvious trip because I had so enjoyed my first weekend getaway at the ocean very much. So did everyone who was there being read. After that first weekend I was flooded with people asking when I would do it again. My heart knew it was time to return to the ocean. I felt at peace about having a chance to read by the waves again. As I said before, the ocean is calming and spiritual and having the opportunity to continue my service there was incredibly important to me.

I could feel the difference in the energy of that weekend before I even crossed the Bay Bridge from Baltimore to Maryland's Eastern Shore. It was if the bridge's wide expanse was more than just a transition from the big city to the long highway that leads to rural Maryland and ultimately the Atlantic Ocean. The drive itself was a peaceful one, passing through the small towns of Easton and Salisbury, surrounded by fields and water with increasing frequency. There was a deepening of self when leaving Baltimore's congested one way streets behind and tuning into the serenity of nature and water that always gave me joy.

When we arrived some of my fans were there, so I sat and had afternoon tea and a wonderful conversation with them. No reading, no work, just enjoying new friends and old and feeling blessed to be with them. I went to my room to rest for a while. Soon after, I met some of my fan club members for dinner just before I was to read. I excused myself early to get changed and to have some prayer time before my group. I felt a pull to leave my room early and so of course, I did. There was a jewelry shop in the hotel, a small but glittery store and I as soon as I came off the elevator I was pulled in the direction of the shop. Before I could even cross the threshold of the door I knew I was walking out with jewelry. I was also quite sure it wasn't for me! As I walked around, admiring nautical baubles and seashore keepsakes, I kept getting shown images of butterflies. Butterflies are beautiful and a special symbol to many people but not something I would expect to find in a shop so close to the ocean where starfish and seashells are more likely to be found. I knew though, that I would be looking for a piece with a butterfly on it. I glanced at one of the locked cases and my eyes were drawn to a beautiful silver bracelet with a charm of a butterfly on it. Yes! And a mental fist pump! I knew as soon as I saw it that this butterfly charm was important and once it was in my hands I couldn't pay for it fast enough.

The room I was reading in was right around the corner and down the hall. I walked with a jaunty step, my heart was lite and free, full of love and hope. I clutched my little bracelet, filled with the enormity of what was to happen and excited by all Spirit had to offer. It was in that moment I felt a young female presence by the name of Olivia.

I walked in as my husband introduced me and could still feel Olivia's spirit with me. She moved toward the back of the room but she had no intention of leaving. As I started passing messages my eyes would glance towards where Olivia was in the back, patiently waiting for it to be her turn. It stuns me sometimes, how Spirit and the other side work. Many times I can see spirits who wish to talk, give way to those who *need* to talk. By some unwritten communication, they decide who has the floor at any given time. Halfway through the group Olivia stepped forward. She said her name and then gave a specific date. I passed this information along to the group, knowing that somewhere, there was someone who had a connection to Olivia. A lady's hand that went up identifying herself as Olivia's cousin, Natalie. Olivia stepped in and told her cousin things known only between them. She explained some of her experiences in spirit, that she wanted to say hello to Natalie and also to the rest of her family. Natalie was listening with rapt attention to her deceased cousin.

Olivia told about her years of battling cancer and how supportive her family and friends were. I knew from her spirit, she was a light for her family and many others. I have to make you aware that sometimes, I only receive glimpses from the other side, small remembrances that are still important to those who are grieving the death of their loved ones. However, Olivia's presence was so powerful and her validations were so strong that I was shook with her convictions. When I handed Natalie the bracelet, I was told it was for Olivia's mom. Joan. Then, a little awkwardly I was told to give instructions to tell Natalie to reach out to me after the group. Perhaps what Olivia needed to say to Natalie was for her ears alone. I knew there would be a private message from Olivia for her mom.

After I finished reading the group, I privately spoke with Natalie and told her I felt the bracelet was a gift that needed to be delivered in person to Olivia's mom. I told Natalie that when she was ready, she could contact me and I would help channel a message from Olivia to Joan. Natalie reached out to me a few weeks later and I passed on Olivia's private message to Joan. Natalie took the words I had written and wrote them in a card for Joan to accompany the butterfly bracelet. I later received a message of thanks from Natalie letting me know the visit to her aunt went well and that she loved her gift from her daughter. It gave her aunt so much peace, something much needed since the passing of her child.

Since then I have a chance to meet Olivia's mom in person. Joan came to a group I was reading and of course, Olivia jumped right in to talk to her mother. The night was full of new validations including specifics about a charity that was started in an effort to raise money in Olivia's honor. Her mom spoke with me that night, thanked me and said she knew in her heart that she was talking with Olivia. The validations were accurate but it was the beautiful butterfly bracelet that sealed the deal for her. It was all the affirmation she could have possibly needed. I could see the peace come over her face as I hugged her.

Olivia's sign of the butterfly is a sign that will forever be entwined in the memories of the many she loved. Now when they see a graceful, colorful butterfly, they know it is not only God's work but it is Olivia, sharing her joy and thoughts with those who love her. Her loved ones continue to honor her through their charity work and so much more. Her message to her family was a celebration of her life and the continued celebration of their own lives. Her spirit was joyful in the knowledge that her family and friends were at peace with the comfort she provided. I too, know of what she speaks, of how it feels to offer comfort to those who need it. Olivia continues to smile about all the good that is being done in her honor and I smile as well.

Guidance from Above

I met my husband Jeff in the year 2004. I remember the first day I saw him as I walked into his restaurant he owned. We still joke about his first reaction to me. As I walked past him the first time and he saw me, I knew I was to be an important person in his life. I was walking in the front door and he came around the corner from the hallway. I still remember the look on his face when his eyes met mine. I walked a few steps past him and thought to stop but didn't. I doubt coyness was part of the problem but the truth was I didn't turn or start up a conversation with him, psychic I may be, but I am still a woman and I didn't know this man. I continued on my way but watched at the corner of my eye as he ducked into the kitchen. I thought of turning around and peeking in and asking him if I there was something I could do to help him. That would have been more forward than I typically would be, so I chose not to ask. Could you imagine his reaction if I would have? Where was Spirit when I needed a nudge in the right direction? I needn't have worried, there would be time in my future to connect with the man who would be my husband!

The next time I saw him I was with friends. It was a busy night at Jeff's restaurant, but his staff had it under control. He had owned the restaurant for just a few months and as any young business man, he was anxious to continue to improve it. Jeff was actually working on painting the back room, not a very glorious job for an enterprising restaurateur, but Jeff didn't see it that way, it was a job that needed doing and if rolling up his sleeves and painting could improve his business, so be it. I didn't even know he was in the back room painting, until a friend who looked a little like she might have had a drink too many disappeared. I felt I need to see if she was okay so I wandered off in search of her. I could see her laughing and sitting on a couch but had no idea who she was talking to. When I walked around the corner, there was Jeff painting the wall. I walked back to them, said hello, introduced myself, and started a conversation.

A little backstory is in order, before I became a Medium I had thought of getting a degree in Interior Design. I am a messy but natural, creative painter. I love colors and enjoy watching the transformation from green to gray or blue to peach so I wasn't even two minutes into the conversation when I asked that if he needed help, I was around.

Once again the urge to help this man was strong. I have never seen someone's face turn the shade of a tomato so fast. I laughed to myself, this grown man blushing with the thought of me helping him paint, but the offer was an honest one and I hoped he took it in the spirit it was intended. The three of us had a nice conversation, Jeff splattered with paint, my girlfriend a little tipsy and me chit chatting with them both. We said goodbye, a bit reluctantly, but it was time to go and Jeff's painting would not get done with an audience.

I few weeks later I was with Sam, another friend of mine. It was late and we were shooting pool, in Jeff's restaurant no less. The company was great and I was enjoying showing off a bit. Growing up there was a pool table in my childhood home and as is often the case, opportunity and the thought of fun caused my brothers and I to learn to play pool. We got really good at the game and I enjoyed the combination of art and skill that learning to play pool afforded me. The night was getting late, and it was close to closing time for the restaurant when Jeff walked over and decided to join in the play. Sam sat out as we played doubles with another couple. Looking back, I can still see him smoking his cigarette trying to look cool.

At one point Sam whispered to me, "He likes you."

I wasn't sure how to answer that, I felt like a school girl, a little giddy with the thought that Sam thought what I did as well.

Afterwards the four of us went to see a movie. The next day Jeff asked for my number. It took him three days to call me per advice from his friend Jim who told him to wait and not look too eager. Ah, the mating rituals of young men and women! I have to say, I was waiting by the phone, hoping he *would* call. He admitted later he wanted to call the day he asked me for my number. It was a whirlwind romance and after that first date it wasn't long until I knew he was the one.

Within eight months we were engaged, and in a year and seven months we were married.

Jeff has complimented me in many ways, pushed me when I needed it, supported me at all times and his blind faith in my abilities allowed me to have the courage I would need to embark in my life with Spirit and as a Medium.

Once I started to see and hear Spirit in my late twenties, I started to remember other things I was told when I was young, including be told about Jeff. I was reminded of a day, just getting back from a church retreat at the age of sixteen when I was shown the first five letters of his last name. I had forgotten about that for so long. As you know, our married name is not an easy one, and those letters did not make a lot of sense to me. The memory didn't come back until we were married for several years. This opened a flood gate and other memories came back to me. I remember I was driving in a car years before we met and the name "Jeff "was given to me. Months before I met him I was shown an image of an engagement ring. Not even a year later we were engaged. This was all not just coincidence, it was aligned. I needed a strong man to be understanding and supporting of my work and serving God. I needed someone who would really be there as a partner. A man I could depend on, someone who believed in me and my abilities. I had not found this in previous relationships. It was nice to finally find an equal partner, and not one full of judgement and disbelief. Jeff is a loving and open person when it comes to belief in different subjects. Those that know him well know of his love and belief in Bigfoot. Now, when it comes to that subject I actually chuckle, but Jeff is entitled to his beliefs as much as I. We both watch his Bigfoot TV shows and I love his enthusiasm about this crazy ape man!

When we were just a few months in to our relationship, a moment came for me to have an opportunity to tell Jeff about being able to communicate with the other side. I wasn't the one who decided the time was right, it was Jeff's grandmother in spirit. One night after the doors were locked and we were the only ones in the restaurant, Jeff had his first spirit connection. It was well needed and long overdue. Jeff was in the back kitchen running the last few things through the dish washer.

I approached him and said, "Someone is here to talk to you."

Jeff nodded absently and answered, "Hold on, give me a minute I'll be right there."

There were many regulars that looked at his place as a second home, so I knew he thought it was one of them.

I said quietly, "No, you can stay right here." Then continued on, my voice a little hesitant, I said, "Your grandmother is here."

His back was towards me, but I could hear sarcasm in his voice when he said the words "Funny, she is dead."

I answered him, "I know. She is standing right beside me."

He turned and looked at me, just before I was about to start validations. He stood stock still with a shocked look on his face, then murmured, "I can smell her perfume."

I was so grateful to Jeff's grandmother in that moment for helping me prove it was her. She needed him to experience something so special as her own scent to help him understand it was her.

Overwhelmed with emotion, we walked into his office because he needed to sit down. I could almost see his legs shake with the need to buckle as he sat on the chair. I continued with validations from his grandmother. She was clear in her discussion with Jeff through me, she made sure that she told me things that were only between the two of them. Understandably, Jeff was very emotional, but I could tell he needed the release his grandmother's message gave his soul. He thanked me and hugged me, his arms a warm weight around my shoulders. There was no judgement from Jeff, just complete acceptance of what happened. I felt a lightness in my heart at that very moment. It was a relief and a joy to be able to share something so important and intimate with Jeff and to know that he wouldn't think I was a nutcase. I think I even knew back then that this was my calling. In the years since then, Jeff's family gives small messages from time to time, and he is always happy to hear what they have to say. I feel in my heart God sent him to me but feel his grandmother had a hand in the matchmaking.

I like to think that day was a blessing from his grandmother for my path I was yet to choose, and her telling him – "You both have our support from here."

God knew he was the man I needed to walk beside me on this road.

It's not always an easy one, but the twists and turns and occasional detours are something I can overcome with Jeff as my supportive partner. As I celebrate accomplishments he celebrates along with me. He is my soulmate on this journey. I can't help but think back on the day we met and smile. God knew then we would be each other's blessing. As we walk hand in hand on this path for the years to come, I will always be thankful for the guidance from above.

Betty's Tea Cup

This next story is the inspiration that drove me to write Gifts from Spirit. It was a pivotal time for me as it was the first time I was guided to listen, buy something and gift it. I grew up in a town in Maryland by the name of Thurmont. It was a small town, where everyone knew everyone, consider Mayberry with mountains! It was a lovely place to grow up and I have many fond memories of the people and places that were a part of my youth. One particular memory is that of a restaurant my mom and I visited all the time. I can't recall the name of the place but I remember the owner's names, Jim and Lolly. They were great "grown-ups", always warm and inviting plus they would let me go into the kitchen when we visited and eat as many pickles as I wanted. Gold star from a pickle-loving kid! I always looked forward to seeing them. Another restaurant I enjoyed going to was called Mountain Gate. It was a staple as I was growing up and was a cherished place I would go to with my grandparents. It still stands today, a rustic looking building with a view of the larger hills, not quite mountains of Thurmont. I still visit from time to time when I'm back home visiting or touring close by.

On a visit back home, I was passing messages to a small group of sixty at a local restaurant about ten minutes from where I grew up. I had a group just across the Pennsylvania line the next evening. Jeff and I decided to stay in Emmitsburg, Maryland since it was a half an hour away from my group in PA that next night. The morning before going into Pennsylvania, Jeff and I decided to go to Mountain Gate for lunch. As we were sitting I heard a lady in Spirit telling me her name was Betty. I politely told her I could hear her and I felt a strong pull that I would be passing a message for her soon. I let her know to come back to me later, that I was at rest preparing for my group that night. I only heard her say her name twice. She honored my time of rest, and down time with my hubby. Spirits can be pushy sometimes, but as I said earlier, they are also very understanding about waiting their line in que. After we finished eating lunch we went to leave. As Jeff was paying the check I wandered through the gift shop upfront. It's rare I find something in this type of restaurant/store, think Cracker Barrel on a much smaller scale. Still, I enjoy looking at the available wares and knick knacks. Always a shopper at heart, I keep my eyes open for that something special. I kept being drawn to the plugin night lights upfront. There was one in particular that caught my eye. It was shaped like a tea pot with a cardinal and blue jay on it. I couldn't turn away from it. It was not my taste at all and it was not something I would purchase to put in my own home. But I felt I wanted it. No matter, I didn't really like it, so why should I worry? Jeff walked towards me and asked if I was ready. I said yes and we started to walk to the front doors. I literally stopped in my tracks, as if I hit a brick wall. This was a new one from Spirit. Physically stopping me from moving?

I turned to Jeff and said, "I can't walk through the door."

A swirling circle of energy came around me, enveloped me, warm, present and insistent. I turned, cocking my head to one side when I heard one my guides say go back and buy the tea cup night light. I looked at Jeff and told him what my guide was saying and that I could not leave without the night light. Jeff looked quizzical, he had never seen or heard this before, but as usual, he didn't try to convince me otherwise. He had learned enough about my conversations with Spirit and enough about my own stubbornness to realize it was a done deal.

We left with the tea cup night light, it's two bright little birds tumbled in gift wrap.

When we got in the car I said this is for someone coming tonight. I already felt it. It did not dawn on me to connect Betty at that point. After all, she had quietly backed off when I asked her to. On our drive to PA I started to think of Betty. It still didn't make much sense. I wasn't sure if it was part of her message or if I would be delivering two separate messages.

When I entered the room to begin to read messages, I could already feel Betty, her presence strong around me. She told me to take the gift from Jeff. I did as asked and then said Betty's name. Her daughter, granddaughter and husband were in the room. I was compelled to offer them the story that lead to me getting the gift. From hearing Betty's name, to the restaurant we were in, to being stopped and guided to buy the gift and to bring it with me that day. I walked over and handed the gift to Betty's daughter. I then passed everything that Betty and Betty's Dad had to say that evening. Her daughter opened the gift while I was reading her. She said in front of everyone that she could understand why her mom, Betty, would pick the tea cup out. She didn't explain much but seemed to know how important the little night light was. After the group that night, like so many other nights, I have a line of people wanting to say thank you or ask questions. The family stuck around until I was done so they could have time with me after everyone else. Betty's daughter Kim came over and hugged me. She asked me if she could pay me for the gift. I, of course, said no. This was a gift, from my hands to hers from her mother.

I was not expecting what she told me next.

She told me that Betty's favorite restaurant was the Mountain Gate. The same restaurant I was sitting in when Betty came to me! She then said her mom drank hot tea every day. I am fond of tea and I drink it almost every day as well and have a collection of tea pots myself, I admitted excitedly. She finally wrapped up the conversation by saying that she knew when she saw the bright, red cardinal on the night light that it was her mom saying hello. She knew in her heart that was a sign from Betty. I remembered how during the message I gave I had told them cardinals were a sign from Betty. And the ever vocal, raucous blue jays was a sign from her grandfather. It made complete sense to us both. I think we were equally in shock, with the possibility of it all happening. How the events of the day had managed to coalesce. A tea cup shaped night light, with a cardinal and blue jay bought in her mom's favorite restaurant. Who knew such a sweet gesture from her mom, could offer such comfort, and validations of memories never forgotten? Spirit knew, of course, they always do. Betty did a wonderful job providing validation for her daughter Kim. She let her know through me, that she was at peace. No longer will Kim need to watch for a living cardinals to recognize that her mom is near. She now has a beautiful light shining in her house, with the proof that her mom's soul shines from the other side. The blue jay and cardinal on that light will always remind her that her dear loved ones are both still with her.

Flowers of Forgiveness

I believe in forgiveness. I also believe it can be difficult for

us to forgive, especially when someone has hurt us. It is only natural

to hold on to those feelings and the ensuing human emotions. But for

our soul and our journey it is best to forgive. It can be hard to do and

many times, has to be done over time in small stages. There is not a

magical prayer of forgiveness. Something that will go "poof" and

we suddenly forgive those who hurt us. It is normal and natural for

us to dredge up those old feelings of hurt and sadness, especially

when the person who we have to forgive, is someone we love. Many

people think they can forgive and they will be set free from the past.

It is a lovely thought, but humans are not necessarily hard wired for

this. It is a process and as we continue in our work of forgiveness,

unresolved feelings often come up. This is our souls' way of saying

there is still work to do. As you naturally let go and move through

this process, it can and will get easier. Allow yourself to feel the

feelings that you feel. Do not dismiss them, those feelings are as

much of God's plan and in our makeup as the beautiful feelings of

love. Allow them in, but let them naturally come and go.

Resolution will occur but not always on a "perceived" time frame. Honor where you are in that moment and your feelings. It's important to forgive others through the process and to forgive yourself as well. This next story discusses the gift of forgiveness. I hope it will help you on your path.

I had a private session with a husband and wife. Stephanie was excited to hear from her loved ones and her husband, James reveled in the connections that Spirit provided. They spent several hours at my home. The reading was bittersweet. Stephanie's dad came through and his strongest emotion was that of sorrow and the need for forgiveness. Stephanie's dad came to say he was sorry. He apologized for not being the best dad, and not being in Stephanie's life the way he should have been. I felt a lot of love from him. There was complete love and sincerity in his words of apology. I could tell how much it meant to Stephanie. Her dad went on to tell me that Stephanie would see him in a dream, and to watch for rainbows. I told her the rainbow was his personal sign of forgiveness for her. Something that would remind her that her father loved her and that he needed forgiveness for his lack of attentiveness as a dad. He also wanted it to be a sign of support from him, that he was on her side. It was his way of saying that as she goes through the stages of forgiveness both of them needed to heal, he would be there. I was so honored to help them both.

The next day was a day off for me. I was upstairs doing laundry, and Jeff was lying down for an afternoon nap. I felt and saw flowers, I then saw both Stephanie and her father's face. I then heard my guide say to expect a gift. Not even ten minutes later the doorbell rang. It went unanswered as I was preoccupied, not with laundry anymore, but with listening to my guides. When I finally walked down the stairs and opened the door, there sat a delivery from the florist. I picked it up and carried it in and sat it on my kitchenette table. How lovely? A beautiful bouquet of bright and cheery flowers!

I read the card noticing quickly that it was from Stephanie and James. A special thank you for yesterday's reading. Oddly enough, my thoughts turned to my guides. Why had the informed me of the gift ahead of time? Why take the unexpected joy of receiving flowers from me? The answer was that I needed to draw the connection between Stephanie, James and her father. I needed to know that these beautiful flowers, were not just from Stephanie and

James but from her father as well. Stephanie's dad had guided her to get the flowers for me. They came from Stephanie and James hearts, but their actions were guided by her dad. It was *his* thank you to me for helping him give the words his daughter had waited years to hear.

I'm sorry.

Those two words can be so powerful. He never had the chance, or should I say *took* the chance, to say those words the way he should have while he was alive. It was important for him to share his feelings, his mistakes and his need for Stephanie's acceptance. Stephanie too, needed to hear her father's apology to allow her to continue to heal.

Stephanie sent me a message a few days later. She and her husband were both on a much needed vacation. She went on to tell me she was visited by her father in a dream. It was a peaceful experience and as is often the case, she could not remember much, but she did know she dreamed of her father. She remembered that we had spoke of that during the reading. Then, the next day, she and her husband were shocked to see a beautiful rainbow. Stephanie was awed and surprised, especially after just having the dream of her father the night before. She took a picture and sent it to me. I was mesmerized with the gorgeous colors red, orange, yellow, green, blue, indigo and violet and the understanding that her father had been a part of sending this message and that he had known ahead of time what would happen.

Stephanie went on to tell me how much peace the message had offered her and that she felt she was on the road to forgiving her father. Stephanie's sign from her dad was a sign of forgiveness and peace for her moving forward. The flowers I received were a message of thankfulness for the forgiveness he could finally ask for. I know as Stephanie continues on her journey, her dad will continue to offer healing and love. They are beginning a new father and daughter relationship now. A different one, not of the body, but of the spirit and filled with the forgiveness and acceptance that both Stephanie and her father need. Stephanie can now have the peace she deserves, and her dad can be the dad he wished to be.

The Abalone Circle

The abalone circle is a simple story of the circle of love and life. Our loved ones are always watching over us, loving us, and trying to make themselves known. Sometimes, we understand their symbols, other times we miss them, but they continue to try to reach out for our attention. They are helping us through everything. They are there when we are at our lowest, encouraging us to be brave and to fight on. They are also there in the happiest of times, including special occasions. I have found that birthdays are one day they always try to let you know they are celebrating with you.

I was shopping in a store with a friend one day. (Yes, readers, I do shop quite a lot!) Abalone has always been very beautiful to me. I love the natural swirl of colors and unique patterns that each piece has. They are only common sea snails, but when their shells are polished and shine they are as beautiful as any gem. I think it also helps bring me back to nature and how wonderful even the smallest of God's creatures are.

As we were shopping I saw this beautiful abalone shell necklace shaped into a circle. I wanted it, and felt I wanted it, but kept laying it back down because I knew it didn't belong to me. Once again, I felt that I needed the necklace and as much as I wanted it for myself, it was not to be. I knew after some consideration that it had to go home with me. I had this overwhelming feeling I would be gifting it to someone.

My next event was a gallery reading in Maryland of approximately 80 people. I took the necklace with me, feeling sure that there was someone who needed the necklace. While I was reading the group, I heard a date of Nov. 21 and that it was a birthday. Soon after, a lady in spirit by the name of Lee came through. She told me her daughter was in the audience and that her daughter's birthday weekend was coming up.

Her mom, Lee, had a beautiful birthday message for her daughter. It was the necklace of abalone that I recently purchased. When I gave her daughter the necklace she took it out in front of everyone. She looked at the necklace and then looked at me very surprised. She asked how I knew? I said I was guided to buy it. She then told all of us that just a few days before she saw an abalone necklace that was almost identical to the one she now held, in a magazine and almost purchased it for herself. I will never forget her face, or the feeling I had in that moment. Once again I felt blessed to have been able to help someone connect to their loved ones. To trust in myself, my guides and Spirit to know when and for whom this special gift was for.

Lee had the chance to say happy birthday to her daughter and give her a birthday gift from heaven. Her daughter now had the opportunity to tell a beautiful story about how her mom gave her a birthday gift from spirit. I, for my part, was happy to help and thrilled with joy for them both. I'm sure you can see the connection. The circle. Lee to daughter, to Lee and back again with me as the Medium that helped them connect. The circle necklace of abalone reflected the circle of love that was shared by these two remarkable women.

The representation of the circle of love in the necklace was a perfect gift. The circle of love, the circle of life continues on, and so do our loved ones. They form circles of love and protection around us all the time. Watch for the signs of circles in your life as a representation of your loved ones love for you. The joy and positive love you send will return to you. Like the circle, it has no beginning or end.

Wings of Serenity

A few years ago, I read a couple privately that had lost their son Jonathan. Jonathan served our country. It is always a special honor when I have a chance to communicate with those who have served. Their souls bring duty, commitment and a sense of pride in their service. The couple had a beautiful reading, and I received a lovely testimony from Jonathan's mom afterwards. I was so proud to give this beautiful couple a sense of closure and the chance to speak with their son.

A little time past and they reached out to Jeff to book a family group, to give others in their family a chance to connect to Jonathan and other loved ones they were missing. Jeff arranged the meeting and all was set.

It had been quite a while since I had seen Jonathan's parents. As I mentioned before, I read many people and I can't remember every one. Jonathan was not about to let that happen to his folks! About a week before their group Jonathan came to me and I, naturally, went shopping! With Johnathan in tow! He had me buy this beautiful framed portrait of a cardinal with an even more beautifully worded poem. The poem was about the sign of the cardinal, and how our loving departed watch over their family. The reading was set for Mother's day weekend and I could hardly wait to give it to Jonathan's mother. When I arrived, before I even started the reading session with them, I felt I needed to give it to her first. When Jonathan's mother held the lovely picture she was amazed.

Jonathan's mom told me about her day the morning of the reading. On her way to pick up food that late morning a cardinal flew right at her window while she was driving. On the way back home from getting the food, it happened again in the exact same spot while she was driving. Luckily, the bird was not injured and it seemed to Jonathan's mom that it was her son, grabbing her attention and making her aware that he was around. It was such great validation to hear.

I think back on the never ending coincidence. Johnathan guided me to get that portrait the week before his family's reading and then just before I arrived that day, Jonathan was still at work getting his mom's attention. His energy affected that cardinal on two separate occasions. It was important to Jonathan for him to reach out to his mother and let her know he was watching his family and waiting to connect with them that afternoon. It was his "Happy Mother's Day" to his mom. The reading that day was full of love and expressions of hope from the family and their dear, lost relative.

A few days later I received a surprise gift from a friend. It was that same poem, with a picture of a cardinal. The only difference was the background, and framing. Could Jonathan have had a hand in this? I think so. Perhaps it was his way of saying thank you!

I say all the time, that famous old saying, there is no such thing as a coincidence. All things are guided by spirit. I love all the ways they work together from the other side. You may never know how they are working in your life and sometimes, it may seem they are not working at all! But always trust that they are. The other side does all they can in small and big ways to let you know they are close.

Ring of Inspiration

A few years ago I had a young girl by the name of Tiffany come to see me. I was still living in the Baltimore area at the time. Tiffany came to see me for a one on one private reading. These are always very intimate sessions and I am able to devote all my energy to the person I am reading. When she walked in she smiled and offered a tentative hello. When I looked at her in that moment, I could feel she was hiding behind her smile. There was much on Tiffany's mind and while the smile was genuine, it was laced with worry and confusion and sadness. I smiled back said hello and welcomed her into my home. As she sat at my table I could feel her nervousness. I knew it was her first experience with a Medium without even asking.

Tiffany admitted she was nervous and that she had never had a reading before. She continued to try and smile but again, her energy told me it was a great effort for her to do so. I told her to relax, and that a reading is always loving. A few minutes into the reading I could feel Tiffany's energy lighten. I knew her pain ran deeper than what you could see on the surface, and I doubt it was something you had to be a psychic to know of. For a young girl she had lost many loved ones. Not only that, but Tiffany herself had also had many hardships and challenges in her young life.

All of this was communicated to me in the reading from her loved ones on the other side. In the middle of the reading, I was told Tiffany had lost hope. She had lost hope in her dreams, hope in her path for life, hope in anything good to come. They explained to me she had lost her faith. She believed in God, but her hardships were overweighing her heart and mind. She couldn't handle the difficulties that life had thrown at her. Tiffany was good, her heart was as well, but her life experiences left her empty and confused. This is common after loss, but I could feel the heaviness in her spirit. She was really struggling just to hold her head above water and carry on each day. I felt as if *this* Tiffany wasn't the real Tiffany, and that she had lost herself in the aftermath of pain and sadness. She told me she hadn't felt like herself in years. I felt and understood her pain.

A few weeks before I had been on another shopping excursion. I saw a ring that had the word "Inspire" on it. It was a simple ring but it's meaning was important to me. Once again, I bought it but knew it wasn't for me to own, that somewhere in the future, this ring would be given to someone who needed it. In the middle of the reading my guides prompted me to get the ring. I went into my bedroom and into my jewelry armoire to get it for her. When I came out I handed it to her and said, "This is for you."

I told her how I was guided to buy it. That I was told it was for a reading and that I had been waiting to see who it belonged to. It belonged to Tiffany. Of this there was no doubt. It fit her perfectly, as if I had it sized in a jewelry shop! It looked beautiful on her hand and I felt a rush of peace and joy.

I then channeled more messages from her loved ones. They went from giving proof of it being them through evidential mediumship, and through the strong words of love from people Tiffany knew. They finally ended the reading by giving words of encouragement to Tiffany. Their words were strong, loving, and inspiring. Her emotions and mine got the best of both of us. Tears of happiness and past sorrows and the joining of our spirits made for a beautiful afternoon. Tiffany had lost all hope – her loved ones gave it back to her that afternoon. I was so thankful for the healing that was offered. I then shared some personal moments from my own life, where I felt hope was lost as well. We bonded over our shared experiences and over those that were different. She kept looking down at the ring and smiling. It was a real smile. Full of joy and hope and promise of the future. I knew when she walked out my door she would have a new lease on life.

I felt Tiffany's soul was set free. I could feel new breath moving through her spirit. I could feel a sense of renewed faith and hope born again. I was excited for her, and what would come in the next chapter of her life. I reminded her to take one day at a time. That's all we can do, stay present, and grateful.

Tiffany has a beautiful reminder of the ring to wear, a tangible connection to something that many consider a myth. It will always serve as a reminder of her time with her family. She can now look down at that ring and know that inspiration for being happy and at peace is everywhere. My message to you, dear reader, is that happiness and peace is indeed everywhere, all we have to do is look for it. I hope this story reminds you to look for your happiness in the smallest of things. Stay grounded in gratefulness and honor where you are now and how far you have come. And of course, where you will be. The future is ours to embrace. Be inspired, and let your inspiration grow.

Family Blessings

My Aunt Trudy has always been one of the most important people in my life. She met my Uncle Bruce a long time ago, but for whatever the reason, they chose not to marry right away. Friends and family had been waiting years for them to tie the knot. Most often, being a Medium allows be to connect with departed loved ones, but being a psychic, I've also been gifted with precognition. In the beginning of the book, I talked about my experience with knowing of my grandfather's death ahead of time. These precognitive events happen with enough regularity that I am used to them. Usually, it is due to a significant event in someone's life.

A few years before Aunt Trudy and Uncle Bruce decide to take the leap and become husband and wife, I saw myself standing beside Aunt Trudy. I understood that she and Uncle Bruce were finally deciding to marry. I did not know the time frame, but I knew it would come to pass.

My life has always been an interesting road to walk, knowing things ahead of time and keeping these precognitive thoughts to myself. Not everyone wants to know ahead of time what their life holds in store. I knew their marriage was coming and I was so excited to be privy to this knowledge.

I remember walking around my house on a day off and I felt I needed to do some tiding up. I could see, in my mind's eye, my aunt and uncle showing up at my door. The next day the doorbell rang out of the blue.

When I opened the door my aunt yelled "Surprise!"

I called upstairs to Jeff to let him know Aunt Trudy and Uncle Bruce were standing in our dining room. He came down and we all walked into the living room. We sat down to talk, and my aunt handed me a box that was beach themed. I smiled, as I always do when reminded of the ocean. When I opened it, there was a note asking me to be a bridesmaid. I was overcome with emotions and started to cry. It made me so happy I could share in her special day in such a significant way. I knew our loved ones were excited about the decision of marriage. I could feel the love of my family in spirit, around me, through me and surrounding me with love.

Those feelings continued over the months to come. I could feel my grandmother, Natalina, with me the strongest. My grandmother had crossed over in September a few years before. She was strong and spoke her mind like a true Italian. Family was always important to her. She was somewhat of a free spirit. She enjoyed traveling, seeing many countries and always taking pictures of her journey's abroad. She loved to tell stories of her travel, and even brought back unique finds as gifts from time to time. My grandmother grew up Catholic and had a very strong faith, something she shared with me during her life.

One of my most beautiful moments was being privileged to be there during her last moments of life. This was to be important to me in more ways than one. Sharing the intimacy of death is incredibly moving and helping someone transition from this world to the next is an amazing experience. It is difficult for me, as for most people, but I have a different perspective on death and dying than most folks.

I had been living in Maine when I received the call from my aunt to make arrangements to come home, due to my grandmother's impending death. As soon as I got off the phone I told Jeff and he got on the computer and started looking at flights. When I talked to my aunt she said they thought my grandmother had around two weeks left and they were trying to prepare our family so we knew what time we had with her. My grandmother was in home hospice and we were grateful that she would be able to spend her final days surrounded by friends and family in the comfort of her own home. Jeff found dates to fly from Maine, one was a Wednesday and one was a Friday. He said how about Friday? I firmly said no and told him to book me for the Wednesday flight. I explained to him I thought Friday would be too late to arrive.

Jeff dropped me off at the airport, and I never gave another thought to why I needed to catch that Wednesday flight. The next day after I got to Delaware where my grandmother lived was spent visiting with my family.

The hospice nurse had come in earlier that day and said she thought it would be at least three days before my Grandmother Natalina died. She went on to say that my grandmother was a strong woman and was not quite ready to pass.

My aunt and I were going through photos, a typical situation to occur when reminiscing on someone's life and certainly with my grandmother's death expected soon. We enjoyed her life in pictures and yet were understandably upset, knowing she would not be with us much longer. My aunt carefully placed the photo album down and said she wanted to take a shower and give me some private time with my grandmother.

I went and sat by Grandmother Natalina's bedside. Her bed was angled in the corner of the living room. It was important to my aunt that even though my grandmother had dementia, that she was in the room with the family. She wanted her to still hear and experience everything that was happening in the home and with her loved ones. Dementia is a horrible condition for both the ones with it and the family who can no longer really communicate with their loved one. It must be noted, that at this point no one in the family knew I was a Medium.

As I was sitting at her bedside and holding my grandmother's hand, I could see my great grandmother Rose and Bruce's mom Lee, in spirit behind my grandmother's bed. I knew they had been watching over her, and that they were there to take her home. I then stepped in and said to my grandmother that my aunt would be okay and that we would surround her with as much love as we could. I could tell she was holding on for her. I also knew she could feel her family beside her, both those in spirit and me. I told her it was okay to go, that we would all be fine. I needed to let her know all of this and to give her the opportunity to transition from life to death. This all took place at around 2:30 in the afternoon.

When my aunt came back down we finished our previous conversation and continued to look through pictures. At around 5:00 a friend of my aunt's who was also a hospice nurse stopped by to visit. I know in my heart she was sent there. The three of us were sitting, chatting and just catching up. Our nurse friend checked in on my grandmother and then looked at my aunt and said that she thought she should make some calls for family to gather. My aunt protested a bit, telling her friend she was told by the other hospice nurse that she expected my grandmother to be with us for the next three days. Her nurse friend told my aunt, she was seeing signs of my grandmother's body shutting down. Being a hospice nurse is great work, and many nurses know, or can sense when someone is ready to let go. There are physical signs, decreases in blood pressure and breathing, but sometimes it is not something as tangible as that. Dealing with death routinely, gives hospice nurses a unique understanding of death and how they can best help their patients and their families.

Phone calls were made and soon the house was full of loved ones. As we all gathered around my grandmother I sat back on the furthest couch from her bed. I wanted everyone to have a chance to be close to her. As I was sitting there listening to last words, and watching everyone's love for my grandmother, a peace came over the room. I then felt an Angel step in beside me. I could see and feel the Angel that was standing on my right hand side. The Angel was easily eleven feet tall, something I was not quite prepared for. I walked to the bed and put my hand on my grandmother's stomach. I felt the gentle rise and fall of her breath. There were two more breaths and then she was gone. Her spirit left her physical body surrounded by love, and I know she felt peace and comfort. My cousin Michael, who I adore, and who has the kindest heart, sat by her side for three hours holding her hand after the last breath. My grandmother passed away at 12:30 am just ten hours after I sat with her and told it was okay to let go. It was my first time being with someone as they passed. I felt a peace that came over me, and I could still feel her presence in the room with all of us. Two very polite gentlemen came from the funeral home and as they walked out of the house my aunt, uncle, and cousin Michael followed. I went to walk with them, but something told me to stop. Perhaps it was my guides, or maybe just my grandmother's spirit. I stood on the front porch and watched the five of them as they stood in a circle and talked. It was a Friday September morning at 3:30 am and the early morning was very dark. Remember earlier in the story when I said that I needed to fly home Wednesday because I felt if I came Friday I'd be too late. If I had taken that later flight, I wouldn't have arrived until after she had passed and I would not have had such a powerful experience being with her during her last moments. I also wouldn't be able to share with what is still one of the greatest experiences I have had as a Medium

As I stood on that front porch standing in that circle with the five family and friends, was my grandmother. She was young and in her twenties. She was glowing white in her beautiful new spiritual glorified body. I only had a chance to see her that way for just a few seconds. It was beyond any words I can express. The beauty of her, the peacefulness that surrounded her and of course, her need to stay with her family in spirit for just few moments more. It is a memory that has stayed with me after all these years and it will forever be a part of me. Those last moments, that last day with her, that image of wholeness she showed me just before she walked away into the light has dictated my need to help those who need help in transitioning from life to death. Of course, nature will take it's course, but death can be a fearful thing and most of us are worried about dying even if it means joining our loved ones on the other side. I feel blessed to be able to understand that death is not an ending but a beginning and that as difficult as it is to let go, the rewards of Spirit and wholeness and release of pain are a true blessing.

Since then my grandmother comes from time to time. Because of my higher understanding of the other side, my loved one's visit rarely. There is no need for them to visit to comfort me, as I am already at peace with their passing. They mostly come to tell me how proud they are of me and the work that I am doing. Sometimes I'll get a message to pass to another loved one. They know that others in my family need their love and guidance, and that my focus is serving as a Medium and helping others.

On one occasion, my grandmother did come to me and asked me to buy a special gift for my Aunt Trudy. She showed me a necklace with two hearts. She then channeled a special letter to my aunt explaining what the hearts meant. It was a gift I gave her at her bridal shower, a special gift from her mother to her daughter during a special loving day, surrounded by family and friends

The two hearts represented the love of my grandparents for her. It also represented the love from Bruce's deceased parents and finally, my aunt and uncle's hearts were coming together as one. It was a symbol of blessing from both sides of the family for the marriage. I was moved by such a beautiful sentiment from my grandmother from the other side.

Grandmother Natalina is still making her presence known and is felt often by many members of my family.

We traveled to North Carolina to enjoy in the beautiful celebration of two lives joined as one during Aunt Trudy and Uncle Bruce's wedding. The day Aunt Trudy and Uncle Bruce got married I could see all the loved ones in spirit from both sides of the family. They were standing in a circle on the beach surrounding all of us. They were there to celebrate and join in on the blessings of the day. As my aunt and uncle celebrated their own wedding vows, they honored their parents in spirit through a special sand ceremony. I could see each of their parents over their shoulders during the celebration. They each chose a special color of sand representing each parent. As my aunt and uncle blended the colors one by one, they each read beautiful statements of love about their moms and dads. I could feel the love, the happiness of their loved one's joy of how they were honored in that special commemoration. I could see their parents smiling, mingling with the smiles of my aunt and uncle. It was a beautiful moment to watch my aunt and uncle and hear their words and it was just as wonderful to see their four parents standing behind them with knowing smiles. I know when Aunt Trudy and Uncle Bruce said those words about their parents, they could both feel in their hearts that their family was with them in that moment.

The celebration continued into the night, filled with laughter, and great times with family. Everyone was there to celebrate the love between this beautiful couple. My aunt and uncle love deeply and when they set their minds to something they do it, they always go above and beyond to express their love in special ways. They are always putting others first. Family and friends who have become family over the years are always priority with them. So, it was in their natural loving style to turn their one-day wedding into a family vacation and a celebration for the whole family. We came from many states all over the United States to be there for that special day.

Some stayed a few days and some were lucky enough to be there the whole week. North Carolina has always had a special place in my aunt and uncle's hearts and they wanted part of their wedding blended with a family vacation.

They made it so!

My aunt said to me - just as the people they love came to celebrate them, she and my uncle wanted to celebrate all of us. It was a great vacation, filled with laughter and great memories that we will all remember for the rest of our lives. We all had such a great time, and there is now talk of doing this every few years. There were many family blessings that week and I am grateful to have been a part of it. I am also grateful to have been able to see and recognize in spirit the family that came to celebrate Aunt Trudy and Uncle Bruce's wedding.

Remember, our loved ones are always sharing in our lives. They are a part of each and every blessing. They also send blessing to us as well. Let yourself be open to receiving blessing from the other side from God and your family. I see blessings as an everyday part of life. Small or large they are always happening. We are blessed in many ways every day. Allow yourself to stop and recognize them when they happen.

Lucky Numbers

Numbers can not only be a sign from loved ones, some think their loved ones help with numbers, or even luck. This next short story is about a couple who started out as clients but are friends of mine now.

I went to Darlene and Butch's house a few years ago to read the two of them privately. Sometimes before I even have a chance to begin the reading I will already be hearing, names and information. Your loved ones in spirit are just as excited as you are for the chance to communicate.

As I was walking up the stairs before the reading, I heard a lady by the name of Adeline. When the reading started, I asked Butch if he recognized her because I could feel her connection to him. He said yes it was his aunt and his godmother. They were very close. I walked into the kitchen and sat down, ready to see what the reading would bring. As other loved ones came through for the two of them I could see Adeline standing in the kitchen in front of the hutch. She waited her turn patiently to step in. When she did, she gave fantastic validation including something I don't often get. She shared her love of horse racing and "Playing the ponies." I could see a racetrack and hear the thunder of horses coming down the home stretch. Adeline told me she would play the trifecta all the time. She then gave her order of the numbers she favored for the trifecta she would play the most. Darlene looked at me and said that they needed to remember those numbers. I agreed! Their loved ones did a wonderful job, sharing time and coming through. I enjoyed my afternoon with them and celebrating connecting with their family and friends.

A few days later I received a message from Darlene telling me that she felt the need to play the numbers Aunt Adeline gave. Not only did she play those numbers, but she decided to play the anniversary date of Butch and her marriage.

They both hit!

She was in shock. I was too! Sort of! I knew the numbers were important but I hadn't expected that! When I got the message, I had to pick up the phone and call her to remind her this was a blessing from Aunt Adeline. Since then that series of numbers has hit many times. The joy Darlene and Butch felt from that gift from beyond will always be a great memory. Not just the monetary gain, but the fact that Aunt Adeline showed her love of her "ponies" in a way that meant something to her. Darlene never did tell me what she did with the gift of the winnings, but I'm sure they celebrated somehow and I'm just as sure Aunt Adeline was in on the celebration in some way.

Numbers can be ways we know we are loved. Whether it's a loved one sending a birthdate or an image of a license plate. Sometimes it is the consistent waking in the middle of the night to a loved one's birth date or date of passing looming on the end table alarm clock. Sometimes it is numbers that would have been shared between the other side and you if you were together in body. Are you a football fan? You may see jersey numbers. Excited about an anniversary? That number may show up again and again. The combinations are endless.

Be open to numbers the other side is sending you. They can be signs of luck as well as sweet memories of dates that are special to you. Pay attention to repeating patterns of numbers, and the synchronicity of how often they happen. This is just one way your loved ones will use to reach out to you from the other side

Keepsakes

There are many keepsakes that we cling to from the items left behind from our loved ones. Furniture, clothes, coins, personal possessions, jewelry and so on. We cherish these connections from the past and even if they have no "real" value, most of us would never part with them.

I was with Jeff's mom one day as she was going through some jewelry she had from his grandmother. She gave me a few pieces saying said she had so much and had no idea what to do with it all. Jeff's grandmother was soon in the room with us, a solid presence that I felt right away. I told Jeff's mom that her own mother could tell me what pieces went to who. She was thrilled I could help distribute the jewelry to family and friends based on her mom's wishes.

She pulled all the jewelry out from many jewelry boxes and started to place it on the bed in front of me. I sat on the bed, and Jeff's grandmother came and stood beside me. She then had me pick up one piece at a time, and I listened to what she said about each piece. She made sure I knew what was to be kept and what treasured

pieces she wanted passed to whom. I would hold a piece in my hand

and she would give me the name of who it went to. It was a lot of

fun and there was some joking along the way about her mom's taste

in costume jewelry. I felt a little like I was playing a combination of

"dress up" and Christmas deliverer, doling out of presents!

It was the first time I had helped with something like that.

I could feel the peace it gave Jeff's mom that she wasn't left

with those decisions. Not knowing what her mom would have

wanted was hard and she wanted to be respectful of her mother's

wishes. Now her mother would have her jewelry passed down to her

daughters and granddaughters in exactly the way she would have

wanted it to be. They will each have a tiny keepsake of her for the

rest of their lives to remind them she is an angel watching over them.

For those of you who don't know, everything holds energy, that

special essence of who owned and loved certain things is especially

strong. So, when we wear a loved one's piece of jewelry, their spirit

can be felt by us, especially if we are open to their love. They are

honored by this from the other side. It makes them happy for you to

enjoy what they left behind. Cherish the keepsakes you have from your loved ones no matter how small or simple. They are memories of love passed to you.

One Love

As I mentioned earlier, my move from Maine to my home state of Maryland coincided with my choice to embrace becoming a Medium. Once I decided to truly dedicate my life to that of service as a Medium, it wasn't long before word spread, and everyone wanted to come and talk to their loved ones. There were several local people from where I grew up that came to see me. The next story is one such story of a Maryland family that touched my heart and still sticks with me.

I read a local family who grew up around the area I grew up in. During the reading, I came to realize that I was speaking with David. Some of David's children and I had even been school mates so it was especially nice to be able to help them connect with their dad. I had several sessions with his daughters, and then a family group. At the family group there was a line formed out the door of people from the other side waiting to talk, but David was always the one his family wanted to hear from. David always reciprocated, speaking to his family whenever he had the chance.

After the group I took two of David's daughters aside. David made me feel, and see a picture in the group but made perfectly clear it was not to be referenced out loud in front of everyone. I went into the bedroom to talk to his daughters privately. I told them that their dad had showed me a necklace with a silver heart. I knew it was a gift for his wife. He gave me a specific date in July that he wanted to celebrate with her in spirit. He asked his daughters to explain it to the other girls and to buy it and gift it to their mom on that day. I told them I felt there would be an inscription to put on the necklace. I told also told them that I would invite David to come back to me to get the words he wanted to express to his wife from the other side.

It took a while before I was able to discuss this with David but I finally had a chance to hear what he wanted. He wanted the words "Two hearts, two souls, one love." What a beautiful, heartfelt message to give to his wife. It was poetic and it was simple but expressed their love for one another, and his love for his wife. I typed the words to David's daughter in a message and waited to hear what would happen.

A few weeks later on that special day in July, David's daughters gave that gift to their mom. They videotaped it and sent to me, so I could see her reaction. I was so surprised they did that. Sending me a video of such a special, intimate family moment? The girls were so excited about giving it to her and were thrilled to be giving their mom a gift from their dad. I understood they wanted me to experience her joy as well. I had a chance to watch her open her special gift and the sharing of that culmination of David's mission was inspiring.

I later received a lovely note of thanks for helping to orchestrate David's loving message. I loved helping a loving father and husband have a chance from the other side give such a special gift. David's wife now has a beautiful necklace as an expression of her husband's love for her. The words of the inscription, so beautiful and close to both of their hearts, brings joy to her. When she wears David's necklace, it will be a subtle reminder of their life together, their shared memories and their love for each other.

Guardian Angel

I have shared many beautiful and intimate aspects of my life as a medium. Now I would like to share a very personal situation regarding me. It is important to share with you and I do it because it shows that I too, am affected by the other side in ways that do not involve readings or buying gifts to share with others.

Jeff and I lived in Maine for four years. We loved living there. We lived in a small town named Ellsworth at the time my guardian angel saved my life. I suffer with hypoglycemia and have for many years. We had gone to bed early that evening. Curled up next to Jeff I had no idea what the night would bring.

It was around 1:00 am and I was sound asleep. I was woken up by feeling someone rub the bottom of my one of my feet. It was enough to pull me out of a very deep sleep. I woke up, laid there for a few seconds, and started to feel very light headed and dizzy. I couldn't think straight. These feelings were typical of low blood sugar and I had been through it before. I knew exactly what was happening. Luckily, I kept my monitor right beside the bed. I had enough focus to check my sugar.

It was twenty-eight.

Twenty-eight is incredibly low, anything under forty is dangerous and can lead to a comatose state. I don't know how I was even functioning in that moment. I had just enough energy to shake Jeff awake. My vision was very blurry and I was extremely weak and could barely walk. I managed to walk down the hall and into the kitchen. Jeff and I are always very proactive with keeping juice, soda, hard candy etc. in the house for my sudden sugar drops. This time was the lowest it had ever been.

Jeff walked down the hall as I was drinking one of my favorites, cherry coke, as fast as I could. He made eggs, ham, toast, and an orange. I wasn't hungry at all but needed to eat to stabilize my sugars. We sat and watched television while I ate and my blood sugar leveled out. It finally was back over three digits and I felt safe enough to go back to bed.

Later on that morning when I got up I felt just fine. I kept thinking of the way I was woken up. It was someone in spirit and now that I could actually think clearly, I knew that it was my high guide who had been watching over me from birth. I know she helped to wake me up. I have had some amazing experiences over the years. I have felt them touch me several times. I am, however, most grateful for that particular time. It saved my life. At a blood sugar level of twenty-eight, if she didn't wake me up, I would have passed in my sleep. I would not be writing these words that you are reading right now.

I'm sitting here now just taking a breath in this moment of realization.

I know I was saved that morning and I have known this for many years and I am thankful for my guides intervention. Typing it out where I am actually visually seeing the words is very profound for me. I have come to understand, that it wasn't time for me to leave at such a young age. That my guides had to step into save me, could in part be so I could be here to be a Medium and serve the way I'm serving. I try to remember that every day is a gift. When I wake up I really try to embrace each day, to breathe it in and feel the joy the day can bring. I truly try to make the most of it. Do I still find myself upset about something silly or frustrated over some issue I have had? Sure I do. I am human after all, but when the day is done,

I am so thankful to still be here to help to serve God and spirit. I think of all the thousands of people I have helped, and the thousands I have yet to reach and I know my job is not complete. I can't even imagine not being here to do this work, this incredible calling. I am grateful for each of you now reading this. You are the ones who have allowed me to share your grief, your growth and your guidance, because yes, I think that the people I read are as important to me, as I am to them.   Thank you for being a part of my experiences. I honor you, and our journey together through this thing we call life.

Jeff's Boy

A few months after Jeff and I got married we adopted a dog. We were out running errands one day and we decided to go to a shelter. Walking through a shelter is always a little heart wrenching. So many deserving dogs and we knew we could only adopt one. As we were walking through, there was a dog I felt very drawn to. A small buff colored "low rider" with eyes like chocolate drops and a short caramel coat.

Jeff's thoughts were mine as well, "He's cute!" Jeff said and I think we both fell for the little guy in a heartbeat.

His name was Howie.

We decided we wanted to spend time with him, so they brought him into the open play room for us. Howie was a character and once we got to know him "in person" we fell head over heal's for the little mixed breed. According to the shelter, he was a dachshund/beagle mix and he seemed to fit the bill. Short legged with a goofy beagle smile and a happy go lucky attitude, Jeff and I knew we wanted him. Howie was three years old with a sad life behind him. He had been found in a bear trap in the woods and would always carry the marks of this horrific ordeal. He also had Lyme disease. None of these experiences caused Howie to be anything other than a sweet, kind little dog and we so wanted to be part of his forever home. He was such a trooper with a wagging tail and dancing eyes. You would have never known the extent of his injuries or the horrors he had been through in his short life.

There was another family who was there to look at him as well. Jeff and I were on pins and needles! We needed to have Howie join our home. The other family looked at him, then asked to see him again as we were frantically filling out the paperwork for the adoption. I felt a little guilty, but a girl has got to do what she has got to do! I'm not sure if I ever filled out anything so fast! I knew Howie was supposed to go home with us.

We won the adoption race and soon we were headed home with Howie! Howie joined our little family, including Jeff's "previous children" a pair of cats named Jackie and Sally. At that time Jeff was obsessed with Tim Burton. If you are a fan of Mr. Burton, you know where this is going but if you don't, watch or re-watch Burton's

"Nightmare Before Christmas." You will find out how he chose

their names. Yup, Jeff is that guy!

On our way home all we could talk about was how would the

cats react to Howie?

It turns out, we were right to be concerned. Sally and Jackie

wanted nothing to do with this…this DOG! It was touch and go for a

bit but Howie eventually won them over.

Sally was our love bug, a large orange marmalade girl with a

tidy white bib, Jackie was a solid orange tabby. Both were our

babies. Jackie was a little more standoffish in typical "I'm a cat,

deal with it," fashion. where Sally would follow me around me all

day if she could. She was constantly under my feet, demanding my

attention. Even though they were Jeff's cats, Sally soon she became

a mommy's girl. Jackie on the other hand was completely different.

She showed love on her terms and was a little more of a loner. When

we had company Sally would slowly warm up to those visiting and

they would become her newest best friends. Jackie would run and

hide, she and wanted nothing to do with anyone but Jeff and me.

These differences meant nothing to Howie, he wanted to be

everyone's friend and slowly he wore them over. Howie was a

gentle soul and they soon all became family. And in typical family fashion, they were each special and individual. While Jackie would always be a little more reserved, Sally and Howie actually became close. They would take naps together on the couch and chase each other in playful moments. When we were living in Maine, we even a bird by the name of Nikki. Nikki would sit on Howie's back and take rides across the room. It was so funny for us to watch. Nikki riding proudly on her chubby little dachshund Howie.

Howie graced our lives for ten years. He ended up bonding with Jeff, even more than me. They were inseparable. Growing up Jeff had a lot of animals, but he would always say that Howie was different. You could see the bond between them, everyone could, it was that special something that sometimes happens between animals and their loved ones. Howie was not just a part of us, but everyone in our family adopted him. Toward the end of his life, Howie began to act lethargic and his movements became slow and painful. Jeff's mom was a nurse and even she made mention of the slowness. It's as if we were watching him walk in slow motion. We wondered if it was neurological, maybe even damage done those years ago in a bear trap? One day he woke up and he couldn't walk at all. We were devastated. We took him to the vet holding our breath through it all. She told us, we could try medication to see how he would do. but she admitted we would probably be right back within a day having to make the same choice of letting him go. We both looked at each other without hesitation and agreed we wanted him to be at peace. It was hard for us to say goodbye in that moment. As anyone who has ever had to make this difficult decision, we knew it was right for our boy. For Jeff's boy. We held him and talked to him as he slipped away, stroking his grizzled white gray face and knowing he had lived a wonderful life with us. We stayed with him for some time before we left. Leaving there without him was so very difficult. But it was just Howie's body. Howie's soul was no longer trapped in a body that was failing. I did all I could to comfort Jeff on the car ride home.

It was a hard night as you can imagine and I rescheduled my reading for the next day to give us both time to heal. We were sitting on the couch that next day just resting and watching television when I felt Howie come sit beside me. I stopped for a few seconds, holding my breath. I didn't tell Jeff what was happening but I looked at him and said quietly, "Come over here for a minute."

I then asked him to place his hand in a certain spot to my left. I told him Howie was right beside me, I could see him and had Jeff put his hand where I saw his head. I only had a chance to have him for a brief minute, but the validation was strong. I held it together to pass the message of Howie's love to Jeff. I then saw Jeff's grandmother step in. Howie jumped off the couch and into her arms in spirit. As I saw her catch him, I could see him as a young puppy, around the age of about three, about the same age he was when we adopted him. I repeated what Jeff's grandmother wanted me to pass to him. She let him know that she would watch out for him on our behalf. I saw them walk away into the light. Our little Howie, safe in the arms of Jeff's grandmother. My guides stepped in and finished the communication. It gave us both peace.

Every once in a while I see Howie in spirit, he comes to visit from time to time. Recently we have been both dreaming of him often, which prompted me to tell this story. I know he loves that we know he is around, because our connection with him is still very strong. This chapter is to honor his life and how he changed ours. Please know how much your animals love you and are grateful to you for your love and dedication to them. Rest assured, they too have a place in spirit as well as in our hearts.

A Husbands Guiding Advice

I have a client who has been with me for years. When I first met Brenda I had a chance to read her privately. Her husband came through loud and clear and made his presence known. I have since then read her on many occasions and it was during another private session with her that her husband started giving business advice. It wasn't something that had happened before but I had to honor his wishes. I repeated what he said and she understood. Then he mentioned about buying rental properties in Florida. He also gave me a time line for Brenda when it came for her to purchase condos. She listened and seemed to realize that this was important to her and to her late husband. Sometime later I found out that she bought her first condo in time that he referenced.

At another private reading her husband told me she would be buying the next condo in the same building and reminded me of the time frame. He said it would come unexpected, and quick. Once again, I dutifully passed his information along to Brenda. Once again, her husband was right. Within the next few weeks the condo right next door to the first one became available, so she purchased it right away.

This condo buying continued to be a topic of conversation over the years. He has led her into buying these properties and at the readings she was told, through me, by him, when the correct time would be for another condo purchase. She has followed his wishes and has profited by his astute business sense.

At the time of this writing, Brenda has five condos and will be purchasing her sixth soon. Her husband is helping to take care of his wife and daughter financially from the other side and he is doing a wonderful job! Of course, Brenda is doing a great job as well, she is managing her successful businesses but her husband is still watching out for what is best for his wife and daughter.

I'm waiting to hear about the sixth property and feel she will continue to grow financially and spiritually with the help of her husband. Brenda feels and sees her husband from time to time and is very open to his connection. I think, in part, this has encouraged her to continue with good business practices. That, and the fact that she and her daughter are benefiting from her husband's spiritual guidance. I am happy to have played a part in the improvement of her financial situation. His guidance and her own increasing business savvy, have allowed her to continue increasing her financial stability and now she is making decisions on her own.

Brenda will never stop trusting what she is shown, feeling her husband beside her for support, and learning to rely on those "gut feelings" he sends her way. The yeah or nay when it comes to condo buying. I know he will be guiding every step she makes with this for many years to come. He has left a wonderful legacy for his wife and daughter to enjoy and share with family, and future generations to come.

For me? I can now add Financial Planner and Business Analyst to my list of achievements! I giggle when I say this, it is tongue and cheek, I am just a part of the conduit that shares vital information from one side to the other. Brenda's achievements are her own an d she deserves all the accolades herself but I know it was her husband's gentle but firm pushes from the other side that gave her the confidence to move forward with her life and her continued financial successes.

A Brother's Hello

I read a small group a few years back at a local restaurant. One
of the gentlemen that came through that night was young having
passed unexpectedly at the age of fifty-five. He acknowledged how
he passed, and his name and a multitude of other validations so his
family knew it was him.

He also gave things they didn't recognize or wouldn't recognize
until they happened.

This is something that happens often. During a reading, I often
pass on information that makes no sense to family members. They
know it is their loved one, because we have already established a
connection and the other side has proved to them through validations
that it is indeed them! Still, random information that appears to have
no discernable connection to them will be stated with clarity. I
always tell my groups that I don't always understand either, but that
I must honor what is coming through and that they may find out
"down the road" what it means. Sometimes, it is a message to
someone else that is connected to them. Sometimes it is just

something that hasn't happened yet. I urge them to remain open and to remember what is being said as the connection does come. In the "heat of the moment" when Spirit is coming through hard and fast, we are often focused on the validations we understand right away. This is expected, but the other side's sometimes vague or not understood messages are as important as the ones we get right away.

In this case, one of the things the man mentioned was to watch for a balloon. He just kept repeating to me about a balloon. He was insistent and I was just as insistent. The family did not recognize it but I honored the validation and moved on to what else he wanted to give with a gentle reminder for them to hold his message in their hearts. I felt when he gave the message about the balloon in the reading, that it would be recognized eventually. I just wasn't sure how or when. Well her brother couldn't have been any clearer.

A few days later I received a very long message of thanks from his sister. Attached to the message was a picture of a balloon! She relayed to me that she went outside to sit on the back-screen porch and to have morning coffee. She saw something laying in the yard, when she walked over to get it, she realized it was a balloon. If I remember correctly, the balloon his sister found had a message on it, like most party balloon do. Happy Birthday or Congratulations! The message her balloon said was "Thinking of you!"

She was so surprised and overjoyed that her brother had somehow, found a way to let her know how much he cared! I loved getting the message and proof of what he was validating that night. Again, I bring up coincidence vs validation. Could this be a simple coincidence? Nope. This was her brother's validation of his balloon reference from the other night. I continue to be amazed at what the other side has in store for us!

During the same reading, the man looked at his other sister and said the number four. I felt it would be a lucky number for her and also one for her to watch for from him. She didn't understand what "four" was about but took my statement about paying attention to heart. Her brother had said four, so four it was. She decided to play the pick four twice and played the number four in sequence.

She hit both times and won two thousand dollars! She sent a message to me to let me know what happened and I grinned at her brother's special messages to his sisters. Both these validations he gave that night, the balloon, and the number four, he gave for a reason. They were small signs, small blessings that he still was lending a hand, and watching out for the family. He left so suddenly, he wanted to make sure their hearts were open and would continue to stay open to the process of connecting to him in spirit. I think he has done a wonderful job so far in keeping the promise of backing up his validations with me and to give proof that he is well and loved on the other side. Also, that it is important to him, that his family, especially his sisters, remain connected to him. These sisters will always have those memories of their emotions the night they were read and the subsequent realizations that their brother gave them proof of his genuine love for them. He will always be reaching out to make further connections as a protective brother. It makes me smile every time I think of this story, and how strong he has impacted their lives since his passing. Their hearts are forever open to the possibility of anything happening and anything being possible because of their brother and his great love for them.

It was a teaching moment, a small take away from what I have learned as a Medium. Allow your hearts to be open to what you may think is the impossible, because through God all things *are* possible.

The Hummingbird Bracelet

I went to read an in-home group some time back. While reading the group a love one came through and validated a hummingbird as a sign for his granddaughter. Her mom was part of the group and it was held in their home, so naturally, the granddaughter was there and her grandfather made it a point to let me know how important hummingbirds were as a symbol of his love. In my mind's eye, I could just see hummingbirds around her. With tiny emerald greens and ruby reds, the rapid beat of little wings completely surrounded her and engulfed her. These tiny energetic birds often symbolize infinity and community. Her grandfather's symbol was very clear.

I told the granddaughter to watch out for signs in nature, especially of seeing hummingbirds, as they were a sign from her grandfather. I also told her they could come in other unexpected ways as well. I explained to her that sometimes the sign can be a picture of a hummingbird that catches your eye, or someone purchases a lovely card with a hummingbird on for you. Thinking a little outside the box is sometimes necessary when you are dealing with the other side. Just because your personal sign is that of a hummingbird, it does not mean you will be accosted by a herd of hummingbirds!

A lot of times these signs or validations are given through guidance from loved ones in spirit through another person. The other side is always looking for ways to grab our attention and it may take the form of a nudge from a friend or family member to purchase a card, a book or tiny trinket. They then give that present to the person who needs the special reminder of love from the other side. I see it all the time and, as evidenced by many of these stories, I am often the one who is "encouraged" to purchase something for someone else. This of course, is not just designated to psychics, anyone can be the vehicle for the other side, even if they are unaware that is what they are doing. Our loved ones are always looking for ways to make connections that you can claim as true representations of their continued love from the other side.

A few days after I read that group, I found out that an aunt had come to visit with the gentleman's granddaughter. She had been shopping few days before and bought herself a bracelet with a hummingbird on it. She had every intention to keep it for herself. She loved the little hummingbird bracelet! Just before she walked into her niece's house, (the gentleman's daughter), she had a strong feeling she needed to give it to her niece. When she got to the house she explained that she had bought it for herself and then gifted it to her niece. She said she felt that it needed to be hers.

Her sister and niece offered each other astonished glances. Neither one had a chance to tell her that they were just told by me during the reading that the hummingbird was a sign from a grandparent for her. When the aunt gave her niece the bracelet they told her what had come through in the session. She realized and so did they, that her purchase of the hummingbird bracelet was guided by above. How truly remarkable! A loving aunt giving a beautiful present to her niece on behalf of deceased, but forever loved grandfather.

I always trust what is given to me from Spirit. Once again, I was proven right. The hummingbird sign was revealed to me and even the unconventional way it could arrive. I made sure that I explained this fully to the family I read, as it was an important message from their grandfather. Finally it was confirmed when the aunt gave her niece the beautiful hummingbird bracelet. This is all the validation I could possibly have hoped for. What a beautiful way for her guardian to reach out, and further confirm to trust the sign he needed her to recognize.

The hummingbird will always be a sign for her to watch for in years to come. Because hummingbirds can represent community, I believe this aspect was clearly represented in the guidance of the handing of the bracelet through the family, the most intimate community we are a part of. Hummingbirds wings flutter in an infinity pattern through the air, quick and busy, they are always looking for nectar, or perhaps the sweetness associated with it. Remember, the sweetest nectar is within the flower, much like the love that lies within us.

This jeweled, bright splash of color tiny little bird is the sign of growing in faith, while your loved ones interweave through your life blessings and love. As the hummingbird weaves the sign of infinity, your loved ones weave their sign of love through the hummingbird.

A Mother's Instinct

I was reading a small group of ten in Belair, Maryland when I met this mom I'm writing this story about.

Anna came from Delaware to see me, and it was her first time with a Medium. During the reading her grandfather told me about how he was watching over her and her daughter. He then told me about her daughter's health, even specifying that the young girl was having seizures. He wanted me to tell Anna that he had stepped in and helped to save her life during one of her seizures. He even showed me exactly what happened down to the details of that day.

Obviously Anna was very emotional in that moment, but I felt a sigh of relief in her heart. It made her happy to know that her daughter had a health guardian on the other side. This would not relieve her of the responsibility of making sure her daughter got the medical help she needed, but just knowing that her grandfather had a hand in keeping her child safe was so very important to her. As a mother, she was the protector and the strongest advocate for her daughter and her daughter's health but doing it all alone made her anxious and the diagnosis of seizures scared her immensely. She was so thankful to me for the message, and all the other messages she received that day. I told her that her grandfather would help in spirit when it came to her daughter's health and that he has a close eye on her. He also made me feel he was guiding Anna as a mom as well.

Recently I received a message from the lady that held the group that is still good friends with Anna. Anna reached out to her to let her know to tell me what recently happened. This was just a few days ago actually. Anna was awoken in the middle of the night for no reason at all . She was sound asleep and all of a sudden in the middle of sleeping jumped up because she thought of her daughter instantly. She ran into her room and her daughter was in the middle of having a seizure. Anna was prepared and knew how to help her child but if she had not been awoken, she would not have known and the situation could have become very dangerous indeed.

I know it was her grandfather coming to her to help. She said she felt his presence as he stepped in with his guiding presence. I could feel the panic of Anna as I read the message, but then, at the same time I could see her grandfather's spirit, and I could feel his presence as well. Once again, he was protecting his daughter and his granddaughter by stepping in when needed. Yes, Anna woke up from a sound sleep and it could be argued that it was a mother's instinct to help and protect her child. But she admits that she felt her grandfather's guiding hand during a very emotional and scary time for Anna and her daughter.

Our gut instinct, mother's intuition or simply a nagging feeling that something needs to be done, should always be trusted. We know on an intuitive level that these feelings should not be ignored, but we need to learn to trust them. Where does a mom gets that "mother's instinct." In part it is the extremely strong connection between mother and child, but it is often supplemented by the other side's push. It's those gut and heart feelings we need to trust and follow more. I'm so thankful for Anna's guidance from her grandfather, and that her mother's instinct kicked in.

This is two times now, that she knows of where her grandfather stepped in and helped during a medical emergency. I'm sure she will say a thousand thank yous to him and it still won't feel like it's enough but rest assured, it is. The other side helps, not for the glory of it, or for the thank you or prayers sent in their direction. They do it for the love. And that is enough for anyone.

Jean's Legacy

In the first few weeks of my Mediumship, I met a woman by the name of Jean. Like many of the people in our lives, our paths were destined to cross. She started out as a client of mine, but before long she was one of my closest friends. Friendships are some of the most important relationships, we as humans, engage in. Some of our friends are on the periphery of our lives, they are important but just not involved intimately in our day to day experiences, other people become pivotal players. As for Jean and I, we started our friendship in brief exchanges over the phone. This lead to an occasional lunch or perhaps she would attend one of my teaching seminars. She became a developing medium that started to study under me. Her abilities were natural, and her faith was unbreakable. She grew up Mormon and, just like me, always had an unwavering faith in God. It gave us the basis for our connection.

Throughout the years our friendship and connection grew strong. She was twenty plus years my elder, but she was a child at heart in many ways. She had so many years of wisdom and was willing to share that with me. Perhaps it was that added maturity that gave her an attitude that said, "I won't take crap from anyone."

I loved that about her, her complete honesty was as much a part of her as was her incredible, unwavering faith. She could be loving and brass all in the same sentence. If you knew her well, you knew to not take anything as a personal affront, she said what she said because she believed it and it was always said out of love. Her honesty and her loyalty was proven over and over again. She became one of my best friends. She would always talk about the ride through life we would have together. She thought she would live until her eighties and I of course, hoped this as well, however when she said that to me I had a sinking feeling that I would only get the privilege of having her in my life for a few years. Not long after that conversation she started to have some health scares.

It turned out to be cancer, that unforgivable, unrelenting plague that has touched many of our lives. Unfortunately, the doctors did not pin point the cancer right away. By the time she found out the diagnosis, those of us who loved her had just a few months to enjoy to continue everything she had to offer.

Jean, in typical Jean fashion, lived vicariously through her children and grandchildren. Despite her horrible prognosis, it didn't stop her from continuing to keep her family and close friends involved in her life. Jean was a free spirit, but at the same time was very grounded. She enjoyed outings with family and friends and could talk your ear off on the phone. We would talk for hours. I remember on one occasion we talked on the phone for over eight hours, gabbing girl-talk and sharing important and not so important things that we were feeling. She was a true friend and just being with her gave me joy. I had a very busy schedule and tried to see her as often as I could but our long phone calls were our way of catching up, and checking in. There were, during our friendship, times we went months without seeing each other. When we caught up again, it was if nothing had changed and we jumped right in with our friendship as easily as an old slipper. I was her mentor, but in a lot of ways I was a student of hers as well. She taught me a lot about the hard knock experiences of her life. I learned from hers, and she learned from mine. There was an unspoken language between her and I.

Simply. We just got each other.

We finished each other's sentences, and simultaneously spoke the same words over the phone all the time. We were on the same wave length often. She was one of my biggest supporters in the beginning. I always knew if I need an ear she was there. I had just a few people I knew I could depend on, and she was one of the few. I miss her tremendously. Her wisdom and guidance are carried in my heart. Her voice still echoes in my soul, and her presence is felt in my spirit. Her life will continue to be celebrated by many and by me in particular.

On the day of January twelfth, I went to see Jean, on what would be my last day with her physically. Family and close friends surrounded her that day. I arrived in the late morning. As I was walking into the building I felt it would be my last time with her. I took a deep breath getting out of the car as I walked over the threshold of the building where I would say goodbye to my dear friend. I walked into the elevator alone and as I pushed the button of the floor I heard one my guides tell me quite clearly "January fourteenth." I knew what they were telling me and I wanted to embrace all I could that day. To remember every nuance of her face and every word she spoke.

I stayed that day for almost twelve hours. Friends and family gathered around her. She was very ill and in and out of consciousness but would occasionally say something. I hung on to her every word. Even in the last few days of her life, she continued to add her two cents in, making sure that she was heard. Her physical strength was going but her spiritual strength never waivered.

She kept telling everyone to go home. But when she said "go home," I knew it had two meanings, she wanted some privacy and wanted her family and friends to leave and enjoy the comfort of their own homes, but I also knew she was ready to go home to be with God. At one point I was the only one in the room with her I asked if she wanted my help, she said yes. I prayed over her, and asked for peace. I knew she wouldn't pass that day because I already knew that day would be the fourteenth but I wanted to honor her last days and make it more peaceful. I also wanted her to know her dear friend was with her. We both knew that death was only a transition but knowing that and facing my life without this wonderful woman was extremely difficult. Walking out of that room that night when the nurses told us visiting hours were over, was very hard. I kept looking at her and stood in the doorway just taking those last seconds in knowing they would be my last seeing her. I left feeling peaceful, and appreciative of my last day with her.

I woke up the morning of the fourteenth in a great mood. It was a day off for me. Jeff and I made plans to go to dinner and a movie with my brother and sister in-law, Dan and Katie. I was not even thinking of the date. We had a wonderful time, enjoying each other's company and laughing at each other's silly remarks. A typical night out for couples. At dinner Katie mentioned Jean's passing. We were sitting at dinner at around 5:45 and she said Jean passed at around 4:30. I was in shock. How had I not known? How could I have been laughing and having a good time when my dearest friend passed? Why didn't I think of the date when I awoke that day? If I would have, I might have gone to the rehabilitation center. Just one more time to sit with Jean . But then again, I knew the night of the twelfth it would be my last time with her. So why in such a day of feeling so wonderful was the date that she would be passing be blocked from my memory? I still don't have the answer for this. But what I have come to think is that my guides and Spirit kept my mind from thinking of her. It was a concerted effort and I wouldn't be surprised if it was spearheaded by Jean.

She had been surrounded by nurses at the time of passing, not family and friends. This was her choice. She chose to save her family from her last moments on this earth. Spirit reminded me how she kept asking everyone to go home. I came to understand she didn't want anyone to see her suffer in those final moments, in that very intimate transition from life to death. She wanted everyone to have good memories of her. She didn't want anyone remembering her "that way."

Much like Jean lived her life, she wanted to leave on her terms. I have peace about that now. I have seen her from time to time, since she has been gone. I have had a chance to pass messages from her as well. She has had a chance from the other side to let me know how proud she is of me, and the work I am doing. I have been happy to help her loved ones get messages from her. I know she is one proud grandmother from the other side, loving her children, grandchildren and her friends alike. I know she rejoices in the celebrations of all of us that continue in this life. We all smile when we think of her and her bright and engaging spirit and take no prisoners attitude. We were blessed to have her in our lives and I was truly honored to have called her my friend. Her legacy will live on for years to come and in all of the lives she touched.

Proof of Angels

I went to read a small group of ten in Dundalk, MD a few years

ago. My regular clients I had read several times through the years

had booked a group with me. They had a few new people attending

including a skeptical son. Despite his skepticism, he was hoping to

be reunited with his grandmother. The group was held at the next-

door neighbor's house.

When his grandmother stepped to the forefront in spirit, the

young man said, "Ask her to tell you, what I have hidden next door."

The young man, ever the cynic, needed me to prove that what I

did was truthful. He had brought an item and put it in a gift bag.

When he arrived at his parent's house he showed his dad. It was a

surprise gift for his mom. He was so certain he had me pegged!

His grandmother in spirit smiled at me. She understood her

grandson better than I. I asked him to get the bag and bring it over

here.

As soon as the screen door shut, before he made it two steps out

of the door, I knew what it the gift was.

I looked at his dad and said "I see an angel. It's in a circle that surrounds it." I remember drawing a picture on a scrap piece of paper, a round circle with an angel on the inside. It was a quick sketch and I'm not an artist, but the drawing turned out to be very accurate.

Our young Doubting Thomas, then came back in the door. His dad looked at him and said to him I knew what the gift was! His dad explained that as soon as he had walked out the door to go next door to get the gift, I clearly described the gift. The son looked at me and asked how I knew. He wasn't being disrespectful or cruel, he just couldn't believe. I answered that his grandmother showed me a picture of gift and I understood it to be an angel. 1. I even described the color of the angel and pose the angel was in. I said she made me feel it was within a circle. A clear circle, that surrounded the angel and the angel was the focal point of the gift. The angel was clearly a work of art. I showed the young man my rough sketch which clearly showed an angel in a circle.

The young man was red faced and shocked, but he brought the gift to his mother and carefully placed it in her hands. He explained he was recently going through things and found a crystal globe. A globe which held a beautiful angel. He had bought it for his grandmother, but he never got a chance to give it to her before she passed away. So, he thought it would be a nice gift for his mom. After all, it was originally intended for her mom! When she opened the gift, her eyes filled with tears and everyone in the room could feel the love.

I laughed to myself. He didn't believe in communication with the other side and was so sure he had a fool proof way of proving I was wrong! Well, his grandmother made sure that I was given a strong validation to prove that I did, in fact, have a special gift. It was a surprise to him but it was a good surprise. It gave him some faith in believing in something beyond here, and what he could see with his own two eyes. We all know that is what the blessing of faith is. To believe, even if you can't touch what you believe in. It is something many of us know but for some, it is something that takes quite a long time to understand. For others, they never understand. All of this is right and good. Not everyone has to believe as I do. Sometimes the other side just has to work harder to get them to understand.

I love the way his grandmother had him leave to get the gift. She did that, so I could tell his dad, the one person who knew what the gift was. His grandmother loved her grandson and made sure that there would be no doubt in his mind that she was with him.

I love this story and the representation of the angel. His grandmother gave proof of the angel to be passed on in her honor. She then gave the greatest proof of angels with her loving message. She is an angel for her family, and watches over them closely. Our loved ones often serve as angels for us. Watch for proof of your angels, they are all around you.

Angels of Inspiration

I have had thousands of moments like these over the years. I chose just a few to tell you about in this book. I am so honored that you have joined me on this journey. That you have allowed me into your lives and that I've shown you glimpses of mine. I hope these stories give proof of the afterlife. I also hope this book gives you inspiration and confidence that your loved ones remain in your lives. When you feel a special need to feel your loved ones, pick up this book and read a chapter or two. I have faith these stories will bring you happiness, hope and light. I am also hopeful this book inspires you to live fully and embrace the love and inspiration your loved ones in spirit have for you. Give this book to someone else you want to help and inspire. Just like I want to help and inspire all of you through these stories of encouragement from loved ones who have been and still are, angels for their families and friends. Your angels will continue to support you and inspire you through your journey. Let them help guide your life, give you hope, and offer a helping hand. Remember to continue to watch for signs and allow your hearts to be open to the possibilities of their connections with you.

Love does not end with the death of the physical body. It never dies and my wish for you is that this little book offers you comfort when you need it. A smile when you are feeling a little low. And ultimately, the knowledge that your loved ones continue to show their love to you each and every day.

Made in the USA
Middletown, DE
07 June 2021